THE TRINITY

CW00951911

THE
TRINITY

HOW
NOT TO
BE A HERETIC

STEPHEN BULLIVANT

Paulist Press
New York / Mahwah, NJ

Nihil obstat:
Rev. Andrew Cole
25th April 2014

Imprimatur:
Most Rev. Malcolm McMahon, OP
Archbishop-Elect of Liverpool
Bishop of Nottingham
30th April 2014

Drawing on p. 14 courtesy of the author

Cover photo by Neil Cippon / beyerstudio.com
Cover and book design by Lynn Else

Library of Congress Control Number: 2014960166

ISBN 978-0-8091-4933-9 (paperback)
ISBN 978-1-58768-521-7 (e-book)

Published by Paulist Press
997 Macarthur Boulevard
Mahwah, New Jersey 07430

www.paulistpress.com

Printed and bound in the
United States of America

We can get no idea of the one God other than by really believing in Father and Son and Holy Spirit.
　　　　　—St Hippolytus of Rome (*Against Noetus*, 14)

For nothing is so magnificent in God's sight as pure doctrine, and a soul perfect in all the dogmas of the truth.
　　　　　—St Gregory of Nazianzus (*Oration* 42, 8)

We are now touching...a realm in which any falsely-directed attempt to gain too precise a knowledge is bound to end in disastrous foolishness.
　　　　　—Joseph Ratzinger (*Introduction to Christianity*, 114)

CONTENTS

ACKNOWLEDGMENTS

In the opening paragraphs of *On the Trinity*, Augustine writes of having "undertaken, not so much to discuss with authority what I have already learned, as to learn by discussing it with modest piety" (I, 8). While both my modesty and piety are for others to judge, this is certainly how I feel about teaching the Trinity to five years' worth of second-year undergraduates at St. Mary's University, Twickenham. If any of them can bear to read this book, they will realize just how deeply indebted it is to those hours we spent discussing everything from *perichoresis* to Pinocchio to pictures of my mother. I am specially grateful to the students whom I taught during the writing of it into the present format: Marcus Bogle, Julia Brown, Jack Bull, Sacha Bynoe, William Currie, Seamus Cussen, Rebeccah Donohue, Berna Durcan, Siobhan Eaton, Katie Hall, Megan Irvine, Ryan Jones, Kieren Kay, Gabby Lastrapes, Claire Negri, Daniel Nunnen, Joe Phoenix, James Roberts, Joanne Rolling, John Stayne, and Olivia Yabsley. In the very latter stages, elements were also road tested on my systematic theology masters' students: Joanna Bogle; Deacon Jim Colefield; Sr. Maria Natella, OP; Nicola O'Callaghan; Fr. Julius Otoaye, MSP; and Hannah Young. Sincere thanks to you all.

Also at St. Mary's, my colleagues have created a fun and creative context out of which to produce something like this. I will single out just four in particular here. Rev. Dr. Paul Rowan persuaded me to teach Trinity in the first place; Professor Peter Tyler convinced me it would still be possible to write books, somehow, even if I took over directing the MA program (which I did, and he was right); Dr. Maureen Glackin unfailingly extended sympathy, patience, warmth, encouragement, and tea during an exciting but difficult year, and Francis Campbell, among much else, has made St. Mary's an even more exciting and fulfilling place not simply to *do* Catholic theology but, much more importantly, to *be* a Catholic theologian.

In addition to the students mentioned above, other friends were generous enough to offer both improving criticisms and motivating compliments on drafts at various rough stages: Br. Joseph Bailham, OP; Doug Beaumont; Joanna Bullivant; and Fr. Gregory Murphy, OP.

At Paulist Press, I am hugely grateful to Donna Crilly, Diane Flynn, Mary Ann Carey, Bob Byrns, and, above all, Paul McMahon and Fr. Mark-David Janus, CSP, for their help and encouragement at all stages of bringing this work to fruition—a process begun, ultimately, with Fr. Mark-David's generously giving a stranger some free books at the CTSA convention in June 2011. "I was a stranger and you welcomed me" (Matt 25:35). Although this is the second of my books to be published by Paulist, it is the first to be written especially for them; the first, I hope, of a great many more to come.

Finally, I dedicate this book to my wife Joanna, who throughout this past year, as in every other year—though mystifyingly unbeknownst to her—"has done everything well" (Mark 7:37), as well as to our little daughters Grace and Alice:

> The human family, in a certain sense, is an icon of the Trinity because of its interpersonal love and the fruitfulness of this love. (Pope Benedict XVI, "Angelus on the Feast of the Holy Family," 27 December 2009.)

Stephen Bullivant
Feast of St. John Roberts
December 2014

INTRODUCTION:
SUPREME SIMPLICITY

This is a simple book about an even simpler subject: the doctrine of the Holy Trinity. This must be simple for the Christian God is "supreme simplicity,"[1] and the Trinity is the Church's most basic description of who God actually is—and who he *needs to be* in order to save us. It is at the very heart of what Christians believe, and very little else in Christianity makes sense without it.

To speak of, or pray to, God as *Trinity* is to use a kind of ancient abbreviation. It is a made-up word, a shorthand way of affirming three statements:

1. There is only one God.
2. The Father, the Son, and the Holy Spirit is each God.
3. The Father, the Son, and the Holy Spirit are not the same.

The great majority of Christian believers would, I think, happily agree with each one of those sentences. They are easy enough to understand. They are not filled with weird-sounding jargon, like *consubstantial* or *hypostasis*. Furthermore, every one of them can be confirmed not just from Scripture, but also from the overwhelming witness of Christian faithful from the first century to the twenty-first. This last point is especially important, since the doctrine of the Trinity stems *directly* from the early Christians' experiences of God. Contrary to popular belief, it is not something that theologians invented to suit their own ends. (As we shall note later, many clever theologians tried to "get around" real trinitarian thinking, but could only do so by denying or downplaying one or more of the above statements). Simply put, the reason why Christians talk about God as Trinity is because God revealed himself to them *as* a Trinity: in their own lives, in the collective life of the Church, and through the Old and New Testaments.

Why, then, do Christians not speak more confidently about the Trinity?

In all denominations there are many dedicated, faith-*and*-works believers who feel uneasy when this subject comes up. It is not that they don't believe *that* God is Trinity, because they do. (Large numbers of them, I am sure, would rather die than deny it.) The problem is rather that they are not quite sure of three things: *what* it means to say God is Trinity, *why* Christians are so certain that God must be, and *how* it could possibly make sense.

This triple lack of confidence shows itself in several ways. Teachers and catechists attempt to dodge or skirt around the subject. Perhaps they try not to mention the Trinity directly so as not to risk awkward questions. Or if it features unavoidably in their syllabi, they hunt desperately for a video, or ask someone else to take the class. (When my wife and I went through the RCIA—the Catholic catechetical program for adult converts—our otherwise well-versed team of lay teachers explained how they always try "to get a priest in to do the Trinity session.") Meanwhile, ministers and pastors regularly begin their sermons on Trinity Sunday with a half-joking disclaimer that they've drawn the short straw this week. They then go on to talk about how, of course, the Trinity isn't really something we can understand or explain—that it's a mystery—and that we must accept it by faith alone. It is no wonder that so many churchgoers simply smile, or shrug, or perhaps even cringe, when asked about the Trinity by nonbelievers, or their own children. Disciples who can happily spend hours in person or (more often) online, enlightening strangers over the *only* correct meaning of this-or-that sentence in Ezra or Obadiah, swiftly run out of words when confronted with, "So how can God be *both* three *and* one?"

Such coyness springs from what is, essentially, a praiseworthy instinct: a genuine desire not to say the wrong thing. Churchgoers recognize how central the Trinity is to Christian life and thought. They realize that to talk about the Trinity is to talk about the inner life of God almighty. And so, from fear of misrepresenting him with

2

"empty words" (Eph 5:6), they prefer to say nothing—or as good as nothing—than to lead others astray.

Heresy is a term that we don't hear as much as we used to. That is probably for very good reasons: it is a harsh, arrogant-sounding word when hurled at others, and often isn't helpful in working toward Jesus' hope that his divided followers "may all be one" (John 17:21). Nevertheless, heresy is what sincere Christians, quite properly and prudently, are keen to avoid. It comes from the Greek word *hairesis*, which means "choice," "opinion," or "decision." In the early Church, a heretic was someone who willfully chose to promote his or her own opinions ("heresies") over and against the established teachings of mainstream Christianity. The opposite of heresy was orthodoxy, which is a combination of *ortho-*, "correct" or "straight," and *-doxa*, "belief" or "praise" (in much the same way that orthodontics has to do with correcting or straightening teeth).

Correct belief holds a central place in Christianity. It is far from being the only important thing, of course (see Jas 2:19). But Jesus felt it was significant enough to devote much of his own ministry to the subject. Early in the Gospel of Mark, we see how the crowds are already "astounded" at Christ's authoritative teachings, well before he performs any miracles. And even *after* he has literally worked wonders among them, the people are still talking excitedly about having heard "a new teaching—with authority!" (Mark 1:21–27). Evidently, these were people eager for true doctrine; who better to hear it from than "the truth" (John 14:6) himself? In the Gospel of John, Jesus gives a number of highly theological, doctrinal talks to various audiences (e.g., John 3:1–21; 6:25–65; 14:1—16:33), which even some of his closest followers find "difficult" to follow (6:60). Toward the end of his time on earth, Christ commands his Church to teach the new "disciples of all nations...to obey everything that I have commanded you" (Matt 28:19–20). So essential is this task, that he sends the Holy Spirit as a kind of guarantor of the Church's orthodoxy: he "will teach you everything, and remind you of all that I have said to you" (John 14:26).

The great majority of Christians do not want to be heretics, whether wittingly or unwittingly. They hope to be orthodox. They desire to believe correct doctrine—which is to say, they want to believe true things about God. And that is why they often go silent when the Trinity comes up. They don't feel confident that what they believe, or what they think they believe, about the Trinity *is* fully orthodox. And feeling as they do, they certainly don't want to lead anyone else astray on the topic either. "For you know that we who teach will be judged with greater strictness. For all of us make many mistakes" (Jas 3:1–2).

The problem is that if this is true of everyone—catechists, priests, pastors, Sunday School teachers, theology students, online evangelists—then nobody ever talks about the Trinity. Consequently, no one ever really learns *what* Christians mean by the Trinity, *how* our ancestors in the faith came to think and speak about God in this way, and *why* it was essential that they did so. Furthermore, the Holy Trinity, the very heart of who God is, the essence of who he has revealed himself to be, and the foundation of "the hope that is in you" (1 Pet 3:15), is passed over in silence. It is sidelined and ignored as something that Christians supposedly cannot, and are not meant to, understand.

The sole purpose in writing this book is to help Christians of all kinds better understand the Trinity, so that they can then help others—Christians, non-Christians, and maybe even some not-yet-Christians—better understand it too. My intention is, to paraphrase Martin Luther, "in the plainest manner possible to say about [the Trinity] as much as is necessary."[2]

To repeat something I have already said (you may as well get used to reading this now; it certainly won't be the last time): the doctrine of the Trinity is very simple. It boils down to three, core Christian convictions:

1. There is only one God.
2. The Father, the Son, and the Holy Spirit is each God.
3. The Father, the Son, and the Holy Spirit are not the same.

In chapters 2 and 3, we will see how the first Christians came to be convinced, very quickly, of each of these statements. Having done so, they needed to find a way of affirming all three of them *at the same time*. That proved, I admit, slightly trickier. It took the Church a few centuries, and resulted in a number of failed, heretical attempts along the way. (In each case, as we shall note, the "heresy"

4

amounted to a denial of one of the above three Christian convictions.) However, in its main points, this is not an especially difficult story to understand—as, hopefully, chapters 4, 5, and 6 will amply demonstrate. Chapter 7 will explore a couple of other issues when it comes to untangling the Trinity, but we can worry about them when we get there.

Before examining the early Church's *discovery* of the Trinity, however, it might be prudent first of all to pause. To talk about the Trinity is to talk about the inner life of God. That is probably not something we should do lightly. We often enough struggle for words when talking about our own inner lives. Asked about our thoughts or feelings or emotions, words can fail us, or come up short, or fail to do us justice. If that is so, how much more cautious must we be in trying to do justice to the "Sovereign Lord, who made the heaven and the earth, the sea, and everything in them" (Acts 4:24)—everything, that is, *including* our selves, thoughts, feelings, and emotions? For that reason, chapter 1 is intended as a gentle guide to how (*not*) to talk about God. Those eager to cut to the trinitarian chase may skip it if they so choose: aside from the occasional "as we saw in chapter 1..." type reference, the book should make perfectly good sense without it. Nevertheless, I advise all readers to at least try reading the first page or two. If you get bored, you can skip ahead in the hope you will enjoy chapter 2 better.

Notes

1. Anselm of Canterbury, *Proslogion*, 23. Quoted from *Anselm of Canterbury: The Major Works*, ed. and trans. Brian Davies and G. R. Evans (Oxford: Oxford University Press, 1998), 100.

2. Martin Luther, preface to the *Large Catechism* of 1529. Quoted from Theodore Gerhardt Teppert, ed., *The Book of Concord: Confessions of the Evangelical Lutheran Church* (Minneapolis: Fortress Press, 1959), 365.

1

MORE
THAN WORDS

Here's a cheerful thought: imagine that the only food you have ever eaten has been bought from a McDonald's. All your knowledge of eating and drinking, and all your taste experiences have come from Big Macs, McNuggets, McFlurries, and those little carrot sticks you can get with Happy Meals. Every word or concept you have to think, talk, or dream about food is patterned on fries, McShakes, and those strangely alluring oblong apple pies that come in a cardboard sleeve. "Happy are those..." (Ps 1:1).

Now suppose that, one day, you are whisked away to the restaurant of one of the world's greatest chefs: Heston Blumenthal, for example. In dish after dish you are introduced to flavors you had never dreamt were possible. Beetroot jelly, bacon-and-egg ice cream, salmon in licorice, snail porridge...nothing in your previous culinary life could have prepared you for this. You are overwhelmed by these strange, astounding new experiences, like nothing you have ever tasted before. More to the point, they are like nothing you could ever even have *imagined* tasting.

The meal is wonderful, almost too wonderful in fact. Your senses have been overloaded. You are spent from striving to keep up, from trying to make the most of each new surprise. The coffee at the end of the meal therefore comes as a blessed relief. Chef Blumenthal makes excellent coffee, but so too do McDonald's. Finally: something you can get your head, and taste buds, around without feeling exhausted.

But here comes Heston, suddenly appearing before you, dressed all in white: "Did you enjoy it? I put a lot of effort into these dishes, and it's important for me to know how people find them. *What was it like?"*

The meal was truly amazing, perhaps the peak experience of your life so far. Naturally, you want to tell him what it meant to you (and later, you'll want to tell everyone you know just how great it was too). However, when you start working out how to put it into words, you realize you're in trouble. After all, all your ways for thinking and speaking about food come from your experience of the McDonald's menu.

One thing you *could* do, of course, is attempt to describe the meal in the terms with which you are familiar. You might say, "That bacon-and-egg ice cream was like a cross between the greatest ever Egg McMuffin and the most perfect McFlurry known to man." Or you could say the snail porridge was as though "someone had distilled the tastiness of a trillion McChicken Sandwiches into every bite." Or perhaps you would compare the licorice salmon to "all the wonderfulness of a Fillet-O-Fish sandwich, times infinity, and to the infinite power."

It strikes you, however, that perhaps Heston may not take kindly to such compliments. Even expressed in these superlative-laden terms (*the most perfect, infinite*), you are still comparing his Michelin-starred cuisine with everyday fast food. You are saying, in fact, that the difference between them is only one of *degree.* His food and McDonald's food are effectively in the same league: it is just that Heston's food is a million (or an infinite number of) places higher up. No matter how delicious McDonald's food is, Heston might still consider having his food described in terms of it—even in such maxed-up terms—false and insulting. But what else can you do?

Well, you could try changing tack entirely. Rather than likening Heston's meal to McDonald's food, why not do the opposite? For instance, you could answer him by saying, "That meal was *nothing at all like* a Supersized Extra Value McNugget Meal," or "Your snail porridge was the *perfect negation* of the entire McDonald's menu." In stark contrast to your first attempt at describing the meal, this drives a clean wedge between it and your previous food experiences: the two are in no way alike. You don't have the words or concepts accurately to describe the meal. And yet you still want to say something true about it. So the best you can hope for is to say what it is not.

However, once again, it occurs to you that this might not go down so well either, and understandably so. He has slaved away in a hot kitchen for hours on end, lovingly crafting a mind-bending array of delights, and all just for you...and the best you can do is say, "Well, it wasn't like a McBacon Roll." Seriously?

Now you really are in trouble. Heston Blumenthal stands before you expectantly, puzzled by the pause. You have no words to describe what you have just experienced. You could barely take it all in while you were eating it; you haven't a hope of talking about it meaningfully and satisfactorily now. And then, suddenly, you realize that that might be the answer.

"Mr. Blumenthal...I...I...I'm lost for words." An awe-filled, reverential silence replaces the awkward one of seconds before. Heston smiles.

You say it best when you say nothing at all.

▲ ▲ ▲

This parable tells us much—*though not quite all*—of what we need to know about talking, and not talking, about God.

The basic problem is this. The great bulk of our words, and thus our means of thinking and imagining things, are patterned on everyday, mundane, physical objects in space. As such, we find it reasonably easy to describe *stuff* in straightforward, literal terms. ("The black laptop I am typing on is sitting on a desk. To the left of it are a red pen, an open Bible, and a yellow USB stick," and so on). However, as soon as we try to talk about more abstract things like ideas, concepts, feelings, or emotions, we swiftly begin to struggle. How often, for example, have we answered a question about how we feel about someone or something with "I'm not quite sure," "I can't quite explain it," or "I find it difficult to put into words"? Certainly, I should find it impossible to fully describe what my wife and children mean to me in literal, direct words. Although I am, undoubtedly, the world expert on *my own* feelings about *my own* family (as you are about yours), I simply don't have the right words to come close to communicating them.

What we often do instead is use figurative, metaphorical, poetic language to give some inkling of what it is we're trying to talk about.

Love is like a butterfly,
as soft and gentle as a sigh.
The multicolored moods of love,
are like its satin wings.[1]

Fellow Dolly fans will agree that this does capture *something* of what love is, or can be, like: beautiful, fragile, and fluttery (although these are all still metaphors, of course). Nevertheless, "love is like a butterfly" is very far from being a direct description. Even as a simile ("*x* is like *y*") the comparison breaks down very quickly: love is not, for example, what the Very Hungry Caterpillar turns into. Note also that this doesn't just apply to feelings or emotions. The best science writing is full of metaphors and figurative images—unobserved cats in boxes, flies buzzing around cathedrals, computers made from meat, and so on—precisely because we find plain speaking and thinking such hard work.

If this is the case with things like food and feelings and atoms, what hope have we of saying something adequate about the "King of kings and Lord of lords" (Rev 19:16)? If we struggle when talking about creatures and created things, how dare we speak of the "Creator of heaven and earth, of all things visible and invisible," *himself?*

▲ ▲ ▲

Maybe there isn't any problem here. After all, Scripture is the word of God, written in human words. And it uses them to tell us about God all the time. Here are just three examples, out of thousands and thousands:

God is love.
(1 John 4:8)

Holy, holy, holy,
the Lord God the almighty,
who was and is and is to come!
(Rev 4:8)

Great is our Lord, and abundant in power;
his understanding is beyond all measure.
(Ps 147:5)

10

Even more to the point, God appears to be perfectly happy using human words to describe *himself*:

> For I the LORD do not change. (Mal 3:6)
> I the LORD your God am a jealous God. (Exod 20:5)
> No one is good but God alone. (Luke 18:19)

The problem is that our understandings of words like *love* or *almighty* or *great* are again patterned on our earthly, creaturely experiences. We might have a rough idea of what it means to have a "great cat," to eat a "great hotdog," or to be a "great football player" (although there's still huge scope for disagreement as to what counts as true greatness in any of these areas). Yet surely, whatever it means for a cat, hotdog, footballer, *or any other created thing* to be "great," that must fall insultingly short of what it means for "the Lord your God" to be so too. So while we can be sure that God *is* great, with our finite created minds, and limited earthly experience, we can have little conception of just how God is great, or just how great God is. "God is above whatsoever we may say or think of Him,"[2] as St. Thomas Aquinas once put it.

The danger comes if we forget this—if we imagine that God is great, or loving, or powerful, or jealous in pretty much the same way that, say, a human being might be those things. By doing this, we end up creating a god, or rather an idol or "so-called god" (1 Cor 8:5) in our own image. We put ourselves on a pedestal, supposing that God is just like us, but a bit better. Nor can we avoid this by saying that, unlike us, God is *super-* or *omni-* or *perfectly* or *infinitely* loving or powerful or whatever. This is, remember, exactly what we tried to do in the parable earlier, describing Heston's food as being like McDonald's, but infinitely or perfectly or supremely *more so*. We risk ending up with a God who differs from us mere creatures—"All are from the dust, and all turn to dust again" (Eccl 3:20)—only by degree. It is as though we could simply take the goodness of creation (Gen 1:31), and by turning it up to eleven, somehow reach up to the goodness of the Creator himself. Of course, we cannot do that, and Scripture itself warns us against thinking we can:

For my thoughts are not your thoughts,
  nor are your ways my ways, says the LORD.
For as the heavens are higher than the earth,
  so are my ways higher than your ways
  and my thoughts than your thoughts.
                                        (Isa 55:8–9)

▲ ▲ ▲

Since our thoughts and words are doomed to fail us, the highest, most fulsome praise we can give will always fall insultingly short of "the Most High" (Ps 91:1). Can we then say nothing that is true or accurate about him?

Again, as we learned in our parable, there *is* something we can say. If all our words and concepts aren't up to the job of describing God, let us just be honest about it. Why not just go through the dictionary saying what God isn't? We can start with "God is not aa (a type of Hawaiian lava)" and end up with "God is not zymurgy (the study or practice of fermentation)." And if we get bored a few weeks in, we can even amuse ourselves by doing it Wayne's World style for a couple of days: "God *is* a nonagon (a nine-sided shape)...*not!*"

On one level, this might seem like an improvement. For again, quoting St. Thomas, "What God is not is clearer to us than what he is."[3] We've guarded ourselves against describing God in terms that are beneath him: well done, us. Yet, on another level, all this feels very unsatisfactory. All we've done is given a long litany of God's nonattributes. Talk about damning with faint praise. Is this really the best we can do?

Perhaps Alison Krauss was right all along. Maybe we *do* say it best when we say nothing at all. Rather than "heap up empty phrases" (Matt 6:7), or tediously list what God isn't, why don't we just shut up? "Be still, and know that I am God!" (Ps 46:10).

▲ ▲ ▲

Far be it from me to denigrate this manner of adoration: it has a long and distinguished history within the Christian tradition. The angel Gabriel, for example, prescribed Zechariah some silent time in preparation for his important task of raising John the Baptist (Luke

12

1:20). Moreover, popular piety has long imagined the "holy night" of the first Christmas to have been a "silent night." Throughout Christian history, there have been holy men and women who, singly or together, have devoted themselves to long periods—sometimes even whole lifetimes—of silence. Shorter spells of silent prayer or meditation are practiced by many Christians, of many different stripes, throughout the world on a daily or weekly basis.

Silence certainly has its place, and being "lost for words" is undoubtedly a fitting expression of wonder and gratitude before the One who is "majestic in holiness, awesome in splendor" (Exod 15:11). We human beings are pretty special ourselves, and our intelligence and language are among our greatest glories. Yet it's still worth remembering sometimes that we *ain't all that.* "So do not become proud, but stand in awe" (Rom 11:20).

On its own, though, silence is, in more ways than one, nothing much to shout about. Christianity just doesn't work as a completely wordless religion. Some Christians can keep silent all of the time; all Christians should keep silent some of the time; but all Christians can't (and *mustn't*) keep silent all of the time. There may indeed be "a time to keep silence," but there is also "a time to speak" (Eccl 3:7). Here we return to a point made earlier. Scripture itself is full to bursting with human words and ideas—our very own, flawed, not-good-enough-for-God words and ideas—*about God.* More to the point, it insists, time and again, that we should be so too:

> Praise the LORD!
> Praise God in his sanctuary;
>   praise him in his mighty firmament!
> Praise him for his mighty deeds;
>   praise him according to his surpassing greatness!...
> Let everything that breathes praise the LORD!
> Praise the LORD!
>
> (Ps 150:1–2, 6)

That is, I think you'll agree, not exactly "shaddap you face."

This is the great paradox of theology, indeed of Christian living as a whole. It is no wonder that those who have—or hope they have—received the Holy Spirit, whether as a gentle breath (John 20:22) or "like the rush of a violent wind" (Acts 2:2), feel moved *both* to treasure and ponder these things in their hearts *and* to glorify and praise God for all they have heard and seen (cf. Luke 2:19–20). They have also been positively *commanded* to "go into all the world and proclaim the good news to the whole creation" (Mark 16:15). Naturally, it is nearly impossible to do any of these things without words or ideas or concepts. And yet the only words or ideas or concepts we have to do them with cannot possibly come close to doing God justice. Tasty though McDonald's food is, we can't build a Heston Blumenthal meal out of McNuggets and McShakes. And "very good" though creation is (Gen 1:31), we can't construct an accurate picture of our God out of creaturely categories: "For my thoughts are not your thoughts, nor are your ways my ways" (Isa 55:8).

Speaking of pictures though, perhaps it is time for another parable—one that might rescue us from the corner into which we (with a lot of help from the Scriptures) have painted ourselves.

What, do you suppose, is this?

I have shown this picture to a good number of different audiences over the past several years. Bemused amusement is the normal first impression. After some reflection, most people agree that the antenna-looking object on the right is some form of flower, perhaps a daffodil or something similar. There is little controversy over the two, worryingly large airborne objects: they are presumably butterflies—although, if your love is like one of *those* butterflies, it might be time to seek a relationship counselor. But what of the strange figure on the left? I have heard many creative guesses—it is an alien, or a snowman, or perhaps Peppa Pig—but no one is ever really sure. "They may indeed look, but not perceive" (Mark 4:12).

"But blessed are your eyes, for they see" (Matt 13:16): it is a drawing of the delightful Norma Bullivant, my mother, by her youngest son, me. Neither of us can remember when it was drawn, though both of us hope it was a very long time ago.

Now, you have probably never met or seen a photograph of my mother. You'll have to trust me when I say that this is not a perfect likeness of her. In fact, it is a truly terrible one. For example, she has arms, and hair, and eyebrows, and knees. Even in her thirties, when this was probably drawn, her legs were not *quite* that thin. On any estimation, it is an extremely inaccurate picture of her. If you happen to see my mother walking down the street, I doubt that you'll now go up to her and ask, "Don't I know you from somewhere?"

Considered objectively, this picture is an insult to my mother. Imagine she and I were in a modern art gallery, and hanging there was this picture, but painted by some trendy young artist. Suppose I said, "Mom, why is there a photo of you in the gallery?" Or what if I did this picture for her now, in my thirties: "Look mom, I've made you this for Mother's Day. I'm really pleased with it. Don't you think it looks *exactly* like you? See how well I've captured your nose!"? Perfectly understandably, I think she would find those kinds of comments very hurtful indeed. If that really is the best picture I can draw of her, flowers or chocolates would be a better Mother's Day gift. For that matter, so would nothing at all.

Why then has she kept this false, insulting image? Why didn't she crumple it up in hurt and anger, and throw it away, all those years ago? Why instead has she lovingly kept it?

Most parents, I expect, have a cherished collection of similarly bad artistic efforts by their children. They have kept them because they were delighted to receive them. Infants are not brilliant artists by adult standards, but they put time, thought, effort, and care into doing the very best job they can. Parents know this. They also know that the resulting pictures are far more than *bad* representations of what mom or dad look like; they are *excellent* representations of what their little children's love and affection for mom or dad look like.

Look again at the image. One day, when I was very small, I decided to draw a picture. Of all the many exciting subjects I could have chosen, I picked my mother. I placed her in a garden, in spring or summer when the flowers are in bloom, and surrounded her with butterflies. I even put what I'm pretty sure is meant to be a big smile on her face. Someone who knew me well at that age—someone "acquainted with all my ways" (Ps 139:3)—would understand instantly what I was trying to convey with my flawed, faltering, and false pen strokes—which is why she still has it after all those years.

▲ ▲ ▲

As we should have learned by now, even the best metaphor or analogy isn't perfect. They don't bear too much prodding or stretching, whether you are comparing love to a butterfly, "the LORD the God of hosts" (Hos 12:5) to fine dining, or religious language to childish scribblings. Nevertheless, they do tell us something.

Our flawed and fragile thoughts and words are not up to the job of giving a full, wholly sufficient description of the Most High. It is God who is the Truth, the whole Truth, and nothing but the Truth (cf. John 14:6, 17), and *not* our witness statements about him. (Incidentally, this is not a failure specific to *religious* thinking and speaking. The great British biologist J. B. S. Haldane once famously said, "Now my own suspicion is that the Universe is not only queerer than we suppose, but queerer than we *can* suppose."[4] If that is true of creation, how much more must it be true of the Creator?)

The life of our saintly medieval theologian Thomas Aquinas

illustrates this point rather well. Thomas wrote book after book of biblical commentary and theology, millions upon millions of words about God. Then toward the end of his life, he had a direct, mystical experience of God himself. After that he laid down his pen, midbook, and never wrote another word. When asked why, he answered simply, "I can't....Everything I have written seems like straw by comparison with what I have seen and what has been revealed to me."[5]

In the following chapters—indeed, perhaps, in the rest of our lives—we will do well to remember this lesson in humility. "For great is the might of the Lord; but by the humble he is glorified" (Sir 3:20). In thinking about the Trinity, we are getting better acquainted with *who* God is—who God has *revealed himself* to be. But you and I needn't kid ourselves that by the end of this book, or even by the end of our lives studying Scripture and theology, we'll know God as well as he knows us. That's what heaven is for: "For now we see in a mirror, dimly, but then we will see face to face" (1 Cor 13:12). For the time being, our sight is hampered by both our own shortsightedness, and the gloriousness of what it is we're trying to glimpse. As another saintly medieval theologian, Anselm of Canterbury, once prayed,

> The truth is, I am darkened by myself
> And also dazzled by you.
> I am clouded by my own smallness
> And overwhelmed by your intensity;
> I am restricted by my own narrowness
> and mastered by your wideness.[6]

However, we mustn't let that stop us trying. Throughout the rest of this book, we will be looking at who God has shown, and described, himself to be: Father, Son, and Holy Spirit. In the next two chapters, we will see how and why the early Christians came to be convinced of this, and how they started to make sense of it. And we'll be doing it exclusively through the medium of words. God is indeed "more than words," as St. Thomas well realized. But note, too, that God let Thomas write over seven million words about him *before* giving him writer's block. After all, "The Word became flesh and lived among us" (John 1:14). God became man, and thought and spoke in human language. And we have it on the Holy Spirit's authority that the languages of "every nation under heaven" can be used to talk meaningfully "about God's deeds of power" (Acts 2:5–11).

So, on that note, "let us be on our way" (John 14:31).

Notes

1. "Love Is Like A Butterfly" from *The Essential Dolly Parton*, vol. 2. (RCA Records-Sbme, 1997), http://www.metrolyrics.com/love-is-like-a-butterfly-lyrics-dolly-parton.html.

2. Thomas Aquinas, *Summa Theologiae*, 1a, q. 1, a. 9. Quoted from the translation produced by the English Dominicans in 1920, and delightfully available online at http://www.newadvent.org/summa.

3. Ibid.

4. J. B. S. Haldane, *Possible Worlds and Other Essays* (London: Chatto and Windus, 1927), 286.

5. Quoted from Simon Tugwell, ed. and trans., *Albert & Thomas: Selected Writings* (Mahwah, NJ: Paulist Press, 1988), 266.

6. St. Anselm of Canterbury, *The Prayers and Meditations of Saint Anselm with the Proslogion*, ed. and trans. Bendedicta Ward (London: Penguin, 1973), 256.

2

MEET
THE TRINITY

Though many today would disagree, theists have traditionally believed that the *existence* of God can be reliably inferred from the natural world. According to Paul, for instance, "ever since the creation of the world his eternal power and divine nature, invisible though they are, have been understood and seen through the things he has made" (Rom 1:20). Modern-day apologists might point, more specifically, to the precise configuration of the laws of the universe (the "fine-tuning argument"), or to the very fact that there is a universe, or anything, at all (the "cosmological argument"). Individual arguments go in and out of fashion, but their basic thrust is the same. Even if the Creator wanted to hide himself from us, creation as a whole, or some particular aspect of it, gives the game away. *That* there is a God, it is argued, can be established beyond reasonable doubt, whether God likes it or not.[1]

However, the idea that this God is *tri-une*—Father, Son, and Holy Spirit—is not at all like that. No amount of outside-the-box, blue-skies thinking could "discover" that unaided. That's the kind of thing that, even if true, would have to be *revealed*. And the reason why orthodox Christianity is convinced that God is *in fact* a Trinity of Father, Son, and Holy Spirit is because it is convinced that God has indeed disclosed this information to us. Furthermore, it is convinced that God has done so unambiguously and overwhelmingly, first, within history; second, within the Scriptures (which are our primary witness to that history); and third, in the life and experience of his Church from Pentecost to the present day. "For what can be known about God is plain to them, because God has shown it to them" (Rom 1:19).

▲ ▲ ▲

As a youngish Joseph Ratzinger—the future Pope Benedict XVI—once stated, "The doctrine of the Trinity did not arise out of speculation about God, out of an attempt by philosophical thinking to explain to itself what the fount of all being was like; it developed out of the effort to digest historical experiences."[2] This makes the point clearly. The history of the doctrine of the Trinity *is* the story of the early Christians making sense out of the "deeds of power, wonders, and signs" (Acts 2:22) they had encountered: "for we cannot keep from speaking about what we have seen and heard" (Acts 4:20). The New Testament—a library of twenty-seven books, all written within more-or-less living memory of the first Easter—is naturally our best window onto the first stages of that story, which is precisely the focus of this chapter.

It is sometimes said that the Trinity is unscriptural; that it was an "invention" by later theologians, without any genuine biblical support. It is true, the word *Trinity* appears nowhere in the Bible (and nor, for that matter, does the word *theology*). Furthermore, nowhere does it describe Father, Son, and Holy Spirit as being *homoousios* or as "three persons in one nature" (both important ideas; we'll meet them again in later chapters). However, as I have said before—and will say many more times before this book is through—Trinity is merely a shorthand way of making three simple statements:

1. There is only one God.
2. The Father, the Son, and the Holy Spirit is each God.
3. The Father, the Son, and the Holy Spirit are not the same.

Each of these claims, we shall discover, is deeply scriptural. This is why, as we shall see later, the mainstream Christian community refused to budge on any of them, in the face of several well-meaning opinions to the contrary. Likewise, "three persons in one nature," *homoousios*, and the mercifully few other pieces of theological jargon we will meet, were all devised to safeguard and explain the witness of the Old and New Testaments: witnesses that themselves testify to the work of the trinitarian God, throughout history, in bringing "righteousness and peace and joy" (Rom 14:17) to humanity.

▲ ▲ ▲

Judaism is a monotheistic—one God—religion. The Jews' heroic refusal to worship nothing and nobody less than the Lord their God set them apart in the pagan multigod ancient world.

> Thus says the LORD, the King of Israel
> and his Redeemer, the LORD of hosts:
> I am the first and I am the last;
> besides me there is no god.
> Who is like me? Let them proclaim it,
> let them declare and set it forth before me.
> Who has announced from of old the things to come?
> Let them tell us what is yet to be.
> Do not fear, or be afraid;
> have I not told you from of old and declared it?
> You are my witnesses!
> Is there any god besides me?
> There is no other rock; I know not one.
>
> (Isa 44:6–8)

Joseph and Mary were Jews. Jesus was a Jew. As a Jew, he knew by heart the opening words of the first commandment: "Hear, O Israel: the Lord our God, the Lord is one" (Mark 12:29, quoting Deut 6:4). This verse, known as the *Shema*, he would likely have prayed every morning and every night.

Jesus' disciples, of course, were also Jews. Necessarily, Israel's revolutionary faith in the Holy One was carried over into Christianity. The New Testament authors are equally insistent that "God is one" (Rom 3:30), occasionally even to the point of sarcasm: "You believe that God is one; you do well. Even the demons believe" (Jas 2:19). Monotheism is taken here to be so unquestionably true, that believing it is nothing to boast about. Everybody who's anybody knows there's only one God.

▲ ▲ ▲

But the disciples were not just Jews. They were Jews who recognized Jesus to be the long-awaited Messiah or Christ: "The one to redeem Israel" (Luke 24:21). The reputed place and manner of his birth (Matt 1—2; Luke 1—2), his authoritative teachings (e.g., Mark 1:22), the healings, miracles, and hope for the poor (e.g., Matt 11:4–5; Luke 4:16–21), his entry into Jerusalem (Matt 21:1–9) and all of what happened afterward (e.g., Luke 24:25–27; Acts 8:26–35)...these, and much else besides, convinced Jesus' band of followers that here at last was the fulfillment of "the law" and "the prophets" (Matt 5:17).

Soon—much sooner than is often imagined—the early Christians began to go further. Jesus' words and actions seemed to go beyond *even* what was expected of the Christ. This Messiah was meant to be "a prophet mighty in deed and word before God and all the people" (Luke 24:19). Nobody was expecting "the LORD God, the Holy One of Israel" (Isa 30:15) himself to turn up. *And yet...*

Let us briefly consider just the Gospel of Mark. This is the earliest of the Gospels. Of the four, it's usually regarded as the earthiest and most restrained depiction of who Jesus is and what he does (what New Testament scholars call a "low Christology"). Mark has, for example, nothing to compare to the full-blown theological claims of John's prologue, or the exalted poetic hymns that Luke quotes from Mary, Zechariah, and Simeon. But even here, Jesus repeatedly says and does things on *his own* authority that, for first-century Jews such as himself, could only be said or done on *God's* authority.

According to the Pentateuch, it was "the LORD your God" who dictated, at length, the Jewish dietary laws (Lev 11). Jesus, however, "declared all foods clean" with a single sentence (Mark 7:19–20). The seventh day was "blessed...and consecrated" as "a sabbath to the LORD your God" (Exod 20:8–11). Jesus, meanwhile, announces that "the Son of Man"—that is, he—"is lord even of the sabbath" (Mark 2:28). Elsewhere, people are healed due to their faith in Jesus himself (5:25–34; 10:46–52). He even declares that he "has authority on earth to forgive sins" (2:10). This latter claim is especially revealing. The scribes, who are experts on the law, are naturally scandalized: "It is blasphemy! Who can forgive sins but God alone?" (2:7). The answer to that question, of course, is nobody.

As we have seen already, "the Holy One" is an ancient Hebrew name for the Lord himself. It occurs throughout the Old Testament, most frequently in Isaiah (some thirty times!), but also in 1 Samuel, 2 Kings, 2 Maccabees, Job, Psalms, Proverbs, Sirach, Jeremiah, Baruch, Ezekiel, Hosea, and Habakkuk. Yet in the very first chapter of Mark, a demon cries out to Jesus: "I know who you are, the Holy One of God" (Mark 1:24). And as we learn slightly later in the Gospel, the unclean spirits know full well who exactly Jesus is (see 3:11–12; 5:6–7).

While Jesus is certainly depicted *as* God throughout the New Testament, it is admittedly true that its authors do not state plainly "Jesus is God," or words to that effect, on very many occasions. This is perhaps because, as Jewish converts, the idea of a human and the "Most High God" (Mark 5:7) being *one and the same* person was a very strange and wondrous thing to imagine—as, of course, it still is!—let alone write down in plain letters. That said, the New Testament books *do* directly describe Jesus as God at several places. The first words of John's Gospel, of course, are the most obvious example: "In the beginning was the Word, and the Word was with God, and the Word was God" (John 1:1). The same point is repeated, near the end, with Thomas's cry: "My Lord and my God!" (John 20:28). Paul writes to the Christians in Rome of "the Messiah, who is over all, God blessed for ever" (Rom 9:5). And 2 Peter is addressed to "those who have received a faith as precious as ours through the righteousness of our God and Savior Jesus Christ" (1:1).[3]

▲ ▲ ▲

The New Testament records the early Christian conviction that Jesus is God, incarnate as a real human being: God in the flesh, crawling and then walking around first-century Palestine, eating and drinking, sleeping and waking, dying and being resurrected on the third day. Nevertheless, throughout the Gospels, Jesus constantly refers to another, *who is also God*: his "Father." To give just three examples, out of two hundred or so:

But about that day and hour no one knows, neither the angels of heaven, nor the Son, but only the Father. (Matt 24:36)

Abba, Father, for you all things are possible; remove this cup from me. (Mark 14:36)

Father, the hour has come; glorify your Son so that the Son may glorify you, since you have given him authority over all people, to give eternal life to all whom you have given him. (John 17:1–2)

There is a Father and there is a Son. Very often, the Son talks about his Father. The Son also talks *to* his Father, and encourages the disciples to do the same:

Pray then in this way:
Our Father in heaven,
    hallowed be your name.
(Matt 6:9)

This works both ways. For at Jesus' baptism in the Jordan, the Father speaks to the Son: "You are my Son, the Beloved; with you I am well pleased" (Luke 3:22). And at his transfiguration, the Father announces to the assembled disciples, "This is my Son, my Chosen; listen to him!" (Luke 9:35).

Evidently, the Father and the Son are not the same. If they can talk to each other, and about each other, then they must be, in some very real way, distinct from each other. Or in other words:

The result is a curious paradox: on the one hand this man calls God his Father and speaks to him as to someone else facing him....Christ must be something other than this Father to whom he speaks and to whom we speak.[4]

With that said, the Gospels are quite clear that there is a remarkable closeness between the two. The intimate relationship between "God the Father" (Eph 5:20) and "God the only Son, who is close to the Father's heart" (John 1:18), is glimpsed most fully in the Gospel of John. For instance:

The Father and I are one. (John 10:30)
If you know me, you will know my Father also. From now on
    you do know him and have seen him. (John 14:7)
Whoever has seen me has seen the Father. (John 14:9)

Much more will be said about the interpretation of such statements
later (especially in chapter 4).

Let's recap. This is where we've gotten so far, sticking exclusively to what the Scriptures, and especially the Gospels themselves,
have to say: first, there is one God; second, Father and Son are both
God; and third, Father and Son are not the same. Each of these statements, as we have seen, is firmly embedded in the witness of the
New Testament writers. Necessarily then, each of them reflects the
convictions not only of the first-century Christians who wrote these
texts, but also of the wider Christian communities who read,
revered, copied, distributed, and cherished them. *And there's more.*

△ △ △

The Gospels and Epistles, Acts of the Apostles and the Book of
Revelation, are unanimous. The Father and the Son do not simply
testify to one another: they point to a third divine figure, one who is
once again distinct from, and yet closely related to, themselves:

> The angel said to her, "The Holy Spirit will come upon you, and
> the power of the Most High will overshadow you; therefore
> the child to be born will be holy; he will be called Son of
> God." (Luke 1:35)
> But the Advocate, the Holy Spirit, whom the Father will send in
> my name, will teach you everything, and remind you of all
> that I have said to you. (John 14:26)
> He breathed on them and said to them, "Receive the Holy Spirit.
> If you forgive the sins of any, they are forgiven them; if you
> retain the sins of any, they are retained." (John 20:22–23)

In the Gospels, the Holy Spirit is an even more mysterious figure
than the Father or the Son. Though very often "on the scene" at

critical moments—not least when Jesus is miraculously conceived, and at his baptism—the Spirit is seldom the direct subject of Jesus' teaching. Nevertheless, the Spirit is mentioned frequently, and it is clear that he too shares in "the power of the Most High," that is, in the power of God. From just the quotations above, for example, it is evident that the Spirit is able to work miracles and make things holy, that he teaches authoritatively (just like the Son himself), and that it is through the Spirit that the Church has the power to forgive sins. To quote the scribes at Capernaum once again: "Who can forgive sins but God alone?" (Mark 2:7).

The Spirit really comes into his own, however, in the period after Christ's death, resurrection, and ascension into heaven. In his last words to the disciples, Jesus promised, "You will be baptized with the Holy Spirit not many days from now....You will receive power when the Holy Spirit has come upon you; and you will be my witnesses in Jerusalem, in all Judea and Samaria, and to the ends of the earth" (Acts 1:5, 8). Thus, at Pentecost, the Jewish festival that commemorates Moses receiving the law, the Spirit was poured out onto the Church, spilling over into the whole world.

> In the last days it will be, God declares,
> that I will pour out my Spirit upon all flesh,
>   and your sons and daughters shall prophesy,
> and your young men shall see visions,
>   and your old men shall dream dreams.
> Even upon my slaves, both men and women,
>   in those days I will pour out my Spirit,
>   and they shall prophesy.
>   (Acts 2:17–18, quoting Joel 2:28–29)

To fully understand the early Christians—not just in the New Testament period, but for centuries later—it is essential to recognize that, for them, the Holy Spirit wasn't merely something they'd been taught about in religion classes a long time ago. Rather, it was something they *experienced* on a regular basis. This much is clear from the whole book of Acts, which narrates in detail just what can be accomplished by those who are "filled with the Spirit" (see Acts 2:4; 4:8, 31; 7:55; 9:17; 13:9). Paul too, as one might expect, is insistent

26

that the multiple *charismata* or "gifts of the Spirit" are both manifest, and liberally shared around, in the day-to-day living of each Christian community (1 Cor 12). Readers who are involved with expressly "charismatic" groups or ministries will need no reminding of this fact. Note, though, that Paul's list of spiritual gifts includes not only prophesying, healing, miracle working, and speaking in tongues, but also teaching, helping others, taking on leadership roles, and evangelizing (1 Cor 12:28). Furthermore, Acts is quite clear as to what a Spirit-filled community looks like, or at least *ought to* look like:

> All who believed were together and had all things in common; they would sell their possessions and goods and distribute the proceeds to all, as any had need. Day by day, as they spent much time together in the temple, they broke bread at home and ate their food with glad and generous hearts, praising God and having the goodwill of all the people. (Acts 2:44–47)

Those even slightly familiar with normal church life will need no more proof of the Holy Spirit's full possession of divine powers than that!

▲ ▲ ▲

The New Testament does not use the later shorthand term *Trinity*. Nevertheless, Father, Son, and Holy Spirit are often referred to in the same breath—and often at pivotal moments. Jesus' baptism in the Jordan, as already mentioned, is the classic example here (see also Luke 10:21; John 14:16–17; 20:21–22; Acts 7:54–56). So significant is the episode, in fact, that Mark chooses it as his curtain raiser. So barely a paragraph into the earliest of the four Gospels, we are introduced to the Father, Son, and Holy Spirit, working together to launch Christ's public mission:

> In those days Jesus came from Nazareth of Galilee and was baptized by John in the Jordan. And just as he was coming up out of the water, he saw the heavens torn apart and the Spirit descending like a dove on him. And a

voice came from heaven, "You are my Son, the Beloved; with you I am well pleased." And the Spirit immediately drove him out into the wilderness. (Mark 1:9–12)

Toward the very end of Jesus' earthly ministry, this time in the Gospel of Matthew, we get further indication of the intimate connection between the three. Christ commissions his Church to "make disciples of all nations, baptizing them in the name of the Father and of the Son and of the Holy Spirit" (Matt 28:19). Among other things, this testifies to the sacramental and liturgical practice of the first Christians. They were using this (proto-) trinitarian formula as the dividing line between who, and who is not, a member of the Church. The same wording appears in another first-century Christian text, known as the *Didache* (the Teaching), which is a kind of short, practical guide for start-up Christian communities: "The procedure for baptizing is as follows. After rehearsing all the preliminaries, immerse in running water 'In the Name of the Father, and of the Son, and of the Holy Spirit.'"[5]

What was said earlier about the relationship between the Father and Son may be repeated about the relationship between all three of them. The scriptural witness is clear that Father, Son, and Holy Spirit are intimately related to—one may even say entwined or bound up with—each other. Witness, for example, the following from Jesus' detailed after-dinner speech on Maundy Thursday: "When the Spirit of truth comes...he will glorify me, because he will take what is mine and declare it to you. All that the Father has is mine. For this reason I said that he will take what is mine and declare it to you" (John 16:13–15). I suggest you read those sentences at least a couple of times, and try mentally to untangle the precise interplay between Spirit, Son, and Father they are describing.

Even so, the three are *still* distinct. As Augustine would later put it, "He who is the Father is not the Son...and therefore he who is the Son is not the Father; and the Holy Spirit is neither the Father nor the Son."[6] Again, here is a sentence from slightly earlier in Jesus' farewell discourse: "When the Advocate comes, whom I will send to you from the Father, the Spirit of truth who comes from the Father, he will testify on my behalf" (John 15:26). We have here the Son referring to both the Father and the Spirit (or "Paraclete," from the

Greek word for helper, comforter, or advocate—see Luke 12:11–12).
The Spirit is said to come from the Father, and be sent by the Son, in
order to be a witness for the Son. Again, the precise relationships
here are difficult to distinguish, but clearly, there are three different
"someones" at play.

▲ ▲ ▲

So where are we?
Well, it might not feel like it, but—just two chapters in—we've
already arrived at somewhere very special. In this chapter, we've
seen how the New Testament teaches three things:

1. There is only one God.
2. The Father, the Son, and the Holy Spirit is each God.
3. The Father, the Son, and the Holy Spirit are not the same.

If you've been paying attention—and quite probably, even if you
haven't—you'll know already why that is significant: *we've seen how
the New Testament teaches the doctrine of the Trinity.* For those three
sentences, each of which we've seen firmly embedded in the testimony of Holy Scripture, are, in essence, what Christianity under-
stands by the word *Trinity.* The understanding of God as a Trinity is
not, therefore, something that the early Church read *into* the New
Testament. Rather, it was something that they directly got out of it.
As we shall see in chapter 4 onward, it was by refusing to deny or
downplay any one of those three biblical convictions that the
Christian community, slowly and by no means easily, found a way of
talking about God that did full justice to the scriptural revelation.

Revelation is a critical idea here. We are focusing in this chapter and the next on the testimony of the Scriptures, as the revealed
word of God. Yet we must not forget that, like a strange wild man
"crying out in the wilderness" (Mark 1:3), the Scriptures themselves
point beyond themselves: to the Holy Trinity's own revelation *of itself*
in and through history. "For God so loved the world..." (John 3:16).
The word of God testifies to the Word of God (Luke 1:1–4; John
20:30–31; 1 John 1:1–4), and both it and he also testify to the
Father and the Holy Spirit. We get a particularly strong sense of the
historical nature of the Trinity's self-revelation—first in history

itself, and then through the Scriptures, which are our surest window onto that history—in the thought of the fourth-century bishop St. Gregory of Nazianzus. We'll meet him again in chapter 5, but for now we must be satisfied with these words from one of his sermons. (Gregory, incidentally, wouldn't have regarded preaching on Trinity Sunday as "drawing the short straw.")

> The old covenant made clear proclamation of the Father, a less definite one of the Son. The new covenant made the Son manifest and gave us a glimpse of the Spirit's Godhead. At the present time, the Spirit resides amongst us, giving us a clearer manifestation of himself than before. It was dangerous for the Son to be preached openly when the Godhead of the Father was still unacknowledged. It was dangerous, too, for the Holy Spirit to be made (and I use here a rather rash expression) an extra burden, when the Son had not been received....No, God meant it to be by piecemeal additions...by progress and advance from glory to glory, that the light of the Trinity should shine.[7]

For obvious reasons, this chapter has focused on the New Testament. However, the New Testament forms only a small percentage of the Christian Scriptures. As the above quotation from Gregory demonstrates, the early Christians were convinced that the Old Testament witnessed to the Trinity just as surely as do the New Testament and life of the Church itself, even if "more obscurely." Those who think—or hopefully now *used to* think—that the Trinity is not even a teaching of the New Testament will no doubt find this claim even more unlikely. But we will see in good time how the Old Testament writings took a central place in the early Church's debates about how to speak properly, or rather orthodoxly, about the Trinity. That is to say, the Christian doctrine of the Trinity—its basic understanding of *who* God is—is, to a significant degree, built out of bricks found in the Hebrew Scriptures and deuterocanonical books. Let us turn now to see how the earliest Christians began to *reread* their holy books, in light of "what was from the beginning, what we have heard, what we have seen with our eyes, what we have looked at and touched with our hands, concerning the word of life" (1 John 1:1).

Notes

1. This is the same idea expressed in the famous statement from the First Vatican Council, that "God, the beginning and end of all things, can be known with certitude by the natural light of human reason from created things" (*Dei Filius* 2). The Council fathers then proceed to quote Romans 1:20.

2. Joseph Ratzinger, *Introduction to Christianity* (London: Search Press, 1971), 114–15.

3. A very clear and balanced consideration of this topic may be found in Raymond E. Brown, *Jesus God and Man: Modern Biblical Reflections* (London: Geoffrey Chapman, 1968), 1–38.

4. Joseph Ratzinger, *Introduction to Christianity* (London: Search Press, 1971), 115.

5. *Didache*, 7. Quoted (with slight modification) from Maxwell Staniforth, trans., *Early Christian Writings* (Harmondsworth: Penguin, 1968), 230–31.

6. Augustine, *On the Trinity*, I, 7. Translation from *The Trinity*, trans. Edmund Hill (Brooklyn, NY: New City Press, 1991), 69.

7. Gregory of Nazianzus, *Fifth Theological Oration* (or *Oration 31*), 26. Translation from Gregory of Nazianzus, *On God and Christ: The Five Theological Orations and Two Letters to Cledonius*, trans. Frederick Williams and Lionel Wickham (New York: St. Vladimir's Seminary Press, 2002), 137.

3

REREADING THE
OLD TESTAMENT

"For so it has been written..." (Matt 2:5). "This was to fulfil what the scripture says..." (John 19:24). "This agrees with the words of the prophet, as it is written..." (Acts 15:15). The New Testament is full of phrases like these. They introduce specific prophecies from the Scriptures, which the earliest Christians were convinced had come true in their own times. In doing so, the New Testament authors were following Jesus' own lead. Throughout the Gospels, he often quotes such scriptural "proof texts" as concrete evidence that he is who he claims to be:

> Then he began to say to them, "Today this scripture has been fulfilled in your hearing." (Luke 4:21)
> Everything written about me, in the law of Moses, the prophets, and the psalms must be fulfilled. (Luke 24:44)
> You search the scriptures because you think that in them you have eternal life; and it is they that testify on my behalf....If you believed Moses, you would believe me, for he wrote about me. (John 5:39, 46)

When Jesus or the writers of the New Testament point to "the scriptures" they are, of course, referring to what Christians now call the Old Testament. It is essential to realize that these Jewish holy books completely dominated the imagination of Jesus and his first followers. They thought and spoke automatically in terms of Old Testament names, ideas, images, categories, and concepts. Perfectly reciting whole passages from Isaiah or the Psalms came as easily to them as quoting Bob Dylan lyrics comes to me. As noted in the last chapter, this is for the simple reason that Jesus and the earliest Christians were Jews themselves, and they took their Judaism very seriously indeed. As Paul reminds the Galatians, for example, "I advanced in Judaism beyond many among my people of the same age, for I was far more zealous for the traditions of my ancestors" (1:14). Hence Jesus' followers, as the first century's momentous events unfolded around them, naturally interpreted them in light of the Old Testament. In Christ, they believed, "God fulfilled what he had foretold through all the prophets" (Acts 3:18). This was the way, the only possible way, in which they could make sense of all that they had "seen and heard" (Acts 4:20). As Gerald O'Collins states,

> Some knowledge of the Old Testament is indispensable for grasping the New Testament trinitarian message and its specifics. The Old Testament contains, in anticipation, categories used to express and elaborate the Trinity. To put this point negatively, a theology of the Trinity that ignores or plays down the Old Testament can only be radically deficient.[1]

However, this process of interpretation worked both ways. For if it is Jesus "about whom Moses in the law and also the prophets wrote" (John 1:45), then it makes perfect sense to (re)interpret "the law and also the prophets" *in light of* one's acquaintance with Jesus, and all that he has said and done. And that is exactly what the first Christians did. With the benefit of hindsight, they noticed a great deal in the Old Testament that they believed pointed to, or prefigured, the *actual* events of Christ's life and death. Isaiah's "song of the suffering servant" is a case in point. If, like Peter at Caesarea Philippi (Matt 16:22), one is not expecting a suffering Messiah, then one might easily skim over this passage. However, *after* Easter, Isaiah's vivid description of "a man of suffering" who has been "wounded for our transgressions, crushed for our iniquities...by a perversion of justice," and whose sinless death "shall make many righteous" (Isa 53:3, 5, 8, 11) takes on a whole new significance (see Acts 8:26–39). Similar things might be said about many other early Christian interpretations of the Old Testament. Witness, for example, the words of a second-century bishop, St. Melito of Sardis:

> Therefore if you wish to see the mystery of the Lord, look at Abel who is similarly bound, at Joseph who is similarly sold, at Moses who is similarly exposed, at David who is similarly persecuted, at the prophets who similarly suffer for the sake of Christ. Look also at the sheep which is slain in the land of Egypt, which struck Egypt and saved Israel by its blood.[2]

What we see is a two-way process of interpretation. The Christian understanding of God is both informed by, and in turn informs (perhaps in a radical way), existing categories or ideas. And this is precisely what happened with the emerging Christian understanding of God *as* Father, Son, and Holy Spirit. We saw in the last chapter how the New Testament witnesses to the one God revealing himself in a threefold way in and through the events surrounding the birth, life, death, and resurrection of Jesus of Nazareth. We shall see in this chapter how the early Christians *began* trying to grasp and make sense of all this, using precisely ideas and concepts taken from "the law of Moses, the prophets, and the psalms" (Luke 24:44). We shall also see how, having itself encountered and been transformed by the triune God, the early Church began finding glimpses of this understanding of who he is throughout these holy books.

Let us examine how, by rereading the Old Testament in light of God's recent (and *ongoing*) self-revelation in history, the early Christians uncovered those "treasures of darkness and riches hidden in secret places" by which, says the God of Israel, "you may know that it is I" (Isa 45:3).

▲ ▲ ▲

We have already seen, in the last chapter, how the Christians' conviction that "God is one" (Jas 2:19) flowed directly out of Jewish monotheism. We also saw how various Jewish titles for the one God (e.g., *Lord, Holy One*) are applied in the New Testament to both the Father and the Son.

In fact, *Father* is itself a classic example of Jesus and his followers' "creative borrowing" from the Hebrew Scriptures. The Old

Testament's most popular name for God, *YHWH* or *Yahweh*, appears, either alone or in combination with other titles, approaching seven thousand times. The metaphor of God as a Father, by comparison, puts in merely twenty or so appearances. Sometimes it is used by individuals, as when the Lord prophesies that the Davidic messiah "shall cry to me, 'You are my Father, my God, and the Rock of my Salvation!'" (Ps 89:26). It is also used in a collective sense. Isaiah, for instance, has Israel declare "O LORD, you are our Father" (64:8). Conversely, Jeremiah has the Lord complain that "the house of Israel" has *not* done so: "I thought you would call me, My Father, and would not turn from following me" (3:18–19).

Of course, *Father* is a title that takes on great prominence in the preaching of Jesus, and in the proclamation of the early Church. Though already embedded in the Jewish tradition, we see how it was really taken up and "run with" by the emerging Christian movement. As in the Old Testament, here too it is used both individually and collectively. Most obviously, Jesus, the Davidic messiah prophesied by Isaiah, speaks constantly of "my Father." Furthermore, even the most casual reader of the Gospels cannot but be struck by the special nature of this Father-Son relationship:

> All things have been handed over to me by my Father; and no one knows the Son except the Father, and no one knows the Father except the Son and anyone to whom the Son chooses to reveal him. (Matt 11:27)
> No one has ever seen God. It is God the only Son, who is close to the Father's heart, who has made him known. (John 1:18)

After he was gone, Jesus' followers preserved the precise Aramaic word that he used to address his Father in prayer: "*Abba*, Father, for you all things are possible" (Mark 14:36).[3] So significant did they feel this word to be, that the Greek-speaking early Christians carried it over into their own prayer lives too: "When we cry, 'Abba! Father!' it is that very Spirit bearing witness with our spirit that we are children of God" (Rom 8:15–16; see also Gal 4:6).

Paul's use of "Abba! Father!" shows how the Old Testament's *collective* use of "Father," quoted above from Isaiah and Jeremiah, was also a feature of the early Christians' development of the idea. Most famously, Jesus teaches the assembled crowd at the Sermon on the Mount to pray to "*Our* Father in heaven" (Matt 6:9). He also advises them that "*your* Father knows what you need before you ask him," and "if you forgive others their trespasses, *your* heavenly Father will also forgive you" (Matt 6:8, 14). While affirming the special nature of Jesus' unique relationship with the Father—"the glory as of a father's only son" (John 1:14)—the early Church was equally sure that it too was "adopted," through Christ, into a genuine form of sonship (and indeed, daughtership): "He destined us for adoption as his children through Jesus Christ, according to the good pleasure of his will" (Eph 1:5).

▲ ▲ ▲

As the early Christians strove to comprehend God's self-revelation as Father, Son, and Holy Spirit, they naturally turned to certain deeply scriptural ways of talking about the Lord's nature and activity. In fact, the Old Testament books very often refer to the one God in plural terms. Most obviously, Christian thinkers were swift to notice that, within the first few paragraphs of Genesis, God says "let *us* make humankind in *our* image" (1:26). And a little later, when "the LORD appeared to Abraham by the oaks of Mamre," he appears to do so in the form of three men. Mysteriously, Abraham only addresses them in the singular: "My Lord" (18:1–3). One would be hard-pressed to infer a full-blown trinitarian doctrine simply from passages like these, and early theologians gave markedly different accounts of *how* precisely they do point to the Trinity.[4] But again, once one has been convinced—for the reasons outlined in the last chapter—that there is indeed a "threeness" about how God is and acts, then seeming hints like these take on a whole new meaning.

This was also true of what you might call "personifications" of the divine activity in the Old Testament. These are poetic ways of talking about a part or aspect of a person *as though* it were a separate individual. Such literary devices are not, of course, confined to Holy Writ. In the song *Achy Breaky Heart*, for example, the heart in question is depicted as though it were its own person: one that can be told things ("Don't tell my heart"), fail to understand them ("I just don't

37

think he'd understand"), and which in its grief and confusion might do something stupid ("He might rise up and kill this man"). What Billy Ray Cyrus means is that *he* is having trouble coming to terms with it all. Describing this in terms of what his "achy breaky heart" will or might do is an exaggerated, metaphorical way of expressing that.

At first sight, that is how one might choose to interpret the Old Testament's frequent references to things like God's Wisdom, or Word, or Spirit. Let us take Wisdom—*hokmah* in Hebrew, *sophia* in Greek—first of all. Struggling to make sense of his misfortunes, Job asks,

> But where shall wisdom be found?
>   And where is the place of understanding?
> Mortals do not know the way to it,
>   and it is not found in the land of the living.
> The deep says, "It is not in me,"
>   and the sea says, "It is not with me."...
>
> Where then does wisdom come from?
>   And where is the place of understanding?
> It is hidden from the eyes of all living,
>   and concealed from the birds of the air.
>   (Job 28:12–14, 20–21)

Notice here how "wisdom" is already depicted as a thing (or person?) that an explorer might seek in various out-of-the-way places. Even if one searches high and low for it, however, it remains hidden from view. This is a powerful poetic way of saying that we cannot fully understand the ways and plan, or "wisdom," of God.

In later books like Baruch, Sirach, and Wisdom itself, this kind of metaphor is developed to such an extent that the Wisdom of God is portrayed as a "person" in her (since *hokmah* and *sophia* are feminine nouns) own right. Take the following prayer attributed to Solomon:

> With you is wisdom, she who knows your works
> and was present when you made the world;

> she understands what is pleasing in your sight
> and what is right according to your commandments.
> Send her forth from the holy heavens,
> And from the throne of your glory send her....
> For she knows and understands all things,
> and she will guide me wisely in my actions
> and guard me with her glory.
>
> (Wis 9:9–11)

Hardly surprisingly, the first Christians interpreted such passages as referring, albeit "in a mirror, dimly" (1 Cor 13:12), to Christ. In turn, the Wisdom literature deeply influenced how the early Christian community understood the nature and activity of the Son. Read the following carefully; what does it remind you of?

> I came forth from the mouth of the Most High....
> The Creator of all things gave me a command,
>   and my Creator chose the place for my tent....
> Before the ages, in the beginning he created me,
>   and for all ages I shall not cease to be.
> In the holy tent I ministered before him,
>   and so I was established in Zion.
> Thus in the beloved city he gave me a resting-place,
>   and in Jerusalem was my domain.
>
> (Sir 24:3, 8–11)

John's Gospel begins, "In the beginning was the Word, and the Word was with God" (1:1). "Word" here is a translation of the Greek *logos*, which also means "reason" or "understanding," and which Jewish thinkers had for many years associated with the scriptural Wisdom. A word is, moreover, precisely what might come "forth from the mouth of the Most High" (Sir 24:3). Slightly further on, John famously states that "the Word became flesh and lived among us" (John 1:14). As you perhaps already know, the Greek verb for "live" here, *skenoo*, literally means "to pitch one's tent." Those from a Greek-speaking Jewish background, which of course includes the authors of Sirach and John, would have no trouble with the idea of God going camping. In Exodus, the Lord instructs the Israelites to build a tent "so that I may dwell among them" (25:8) on their journey through the wilderness. In the ancient Greek translation of the Jewish Scriptures, known as the Septuagint, the word used for "tent" here is *skēnē*.[5] This is the same one used in Sirach, and is the root of the verb John employs. Note also that in Sirach, Wisdom's "resting place" is "the beloved city" Jerusalem (24:11). It cannot escape Christians' attention that Jesus, the Word of God, was laid to rest in that dearly beloved city over which he famously "wept" (Luke 19:41).

▲ ▲ ▲

Given the clear parallels between John's Prologue and Sirach's descriptions of Wisdom, it is interesting to speculate why John used the name *Word* rather than *Wisdom* here. Possibly it was because Wisdom in Greek (*Sophia*)—as in Hebrew (*Hokmah*)—is a feminine noun, which is why Sirach refers to Wisdom as "she" above. It would then have been awkward to have "Lady Wisdom" being not only the preexistent Son of God, but also taking flesh in Mary's womb as a little baby boy. This is an interesting topic in itself, which we will address in more detail in chapter 7.

The "word" of God is also an idea that is firmly embedded in the Jewish Scriptures. For example, the Book of Wisdom itself draws a parallel between the creative powers of God's "word" and "wisdom":

O God of my ancestors and Lord of mercy,
who have made all things by your word,
and by your wisdom have formed humankind.
(Wis 9:1–2)

John, of course, affirms that "all things came into being" through the Word (1:3). Furthermore, in Isaiah, just after the "my thoughts are not your thoughts," which we made much of in chapter 1 (55:8–9), comes the following:

For as the rain and the snow come down from heaven,
and do not return there until they have watered the earth,
making it bring forth and sprout,
giving seed to the sower and bread to the eater,

40

so shall my word be that goes out from my mouth;
it shall not return to me empty,
but it shall accomplish that which I purpose,
and succeed in the thing for which I sent it. (55:10–11)

Here, the divine "word" is being sent down from heaven to do a specific mission, only returning once it has been completed.

Now this might be understood as simply an *Achy Breaky Heart*-style personification: talk of God's "word" is merely a poetic way of talking about God's *own* actions. In the same way, I might say to my students, "If you don't get your essays done in time, you will kindle my Wrath. And my Wrath will seek you out, and hunt you down, and pursue you to your homes—and woe to those who do not fear my Wrath!" What I *really* mean, disappointingly, is something like: "If you don't get your essays done in time, I'll be mildly annoyed and inconvenienced. I'll probably even send you a curt email about it. And if you don't get it done within a couple of weeks, then you'll get your grade deducted." But all that sounds far richer and more impressive when expressed using my metaphorical, personified "Wrath." However, the early Christians were convinced that Jesus had *actually* been sent down from heaven, in order to accomplish a specific task for the Father: "For I have come down from heaven, not to do my own will, but the will of him who sent me" (John 6:38); "My food is to do the will of him who sent me and to complete his work" (John 4:34). And having done so, he had now returned (John 20:17; Acts 1:6–11). Naturally, this cast the passage from Isaiah in a whole different light. What might once have been viewed as a literary flourish was now *re*read as a prophecy of the Son's incarnation, mission of salvation, and ascension into heaven. Seen in that light, the mentions in the passages above of life-giving water coming from heaven (cf. John 4:13–14), bread (cf. John 6:32–35), and sowers (cf. John 4:35–38; Matt 13:1–9) also take on much fuller meanings.

Incidentally, we see here again the "two-way street" of interpretation. These existing Old Testament ideas are used to make sense of Jesus' life, teaching, and significance *at the same time as* Jesus' life, teaching, and significance are being used to develop and expand these existing Old Testament ideas.

THE TRINITY

▲ ▲ ▲

To give one final example, the same is very much the case with *spirit*, which occurs some four hundred times in the Old Testament. The Hebrew (*ruah*) and Greek (*pneuma*) words can carry a range of meanings, including "wind" and "breath," allowing some suggestive wordplays largely lost in translation. Thus, Jesus' remark, that the *pneuma* "blows where it chooses...you do not know where it comes from or where it goes" (John 3:8), is a profound theological statement disguised as a comment on the weather.[6] Likewise, his *breathing* on the disciples as they "receive the Holy Spirit" (John 20:22) is more richly symbolic than a simple invasion of personal space. The Old Testament echoes of both episodes would scarcely have been lost on our "rabbi" (John 1:38) from Nazareth. The very first sentence of Genesis describes the spirit—or "wind"—"from God" blowing over the whole of creation (1:2), and it is the "breath"—or spirit—"of life" by which Adam is made "a living being" in Genesis 2:7.

Elsewhere in the Old Testament, "the spirit of the Lord" is present in those doing God's work, as famously when "the spirit of the LORD took possession of Gideon; and he sounded the trumpet" (Judg 6:34), or when Samuel anoints David "and the spirit of the LORD came mightily upon David from that day forward" (1 Sam 16:13). This happens most frequently in the case of prophecy. Indeed, what is said about the seventy elders applies to a great many Old Testament figures: "When the spirit rested upon them, they prophesied" (Num 11:25). Hence the true prophet, Micah, contrasting himself with the false "prophets" leading Israel astray, speaks of being "filled with power, with the spirit of the LORD, with justice and might" (Mic 3:8).

The continuity between the Old and New Testaments on this issue is clear. For the early Church, the "spirit of the Lord" at work throughout the history of Israel, whose inspiration was evident throughout the Jewish Scriptures, was the exact same "Holy Spirit" whom Jesus had breathed onto the apostles:

No prophecy of scripture is a matter of one's own interpretation, because no prophecy ever came by human will, but men and women moved by the Holy Spirit spoke from God. (2 Pet 1:20–21)

As noted in the previous chapter, the first Christians understood themselves to be living out a direct fulfillment of God's promise via the prophet Joel: "I will pour out my Spirit upon all flesh" (Joel 2:28; Acts 2:17). Thus filled with the Spirit, they were able to prophesy and exhibit other such "manifestation[s] of the Spirit" (1 Cor 12:7) just as had "the prophets of old" (Mark 6:15). As far as the early Christians were concerned—although, of course, not everyone always believed them (see Acts 2:13)—it was "one and the same Spirit" (1 Cor 12:11) who was both present at Creation (Gen 1:2), and who was and is at work within the "new creation" (Gal 6:15) in Christ Jesus.

▲ ▲ ▲

One of this book's central claims is that what Christianity means, and what most Christians *want* to mean, by the word *Trinity* is a deeply, solidly scriptural idea. This comes out most clearly, of course, in the New Testament, which is only about one-fifth of the Christian Scriptures. Ignoring the other four-fifths entirely would be a serious omission: what the writers of the New Testament *meant* by the term *Scriptures* is what we now call the old one.

Time and again, we have seen how the New Testament's witness to God's self-revelation as Father, Son, and Holy Spirit is recognized, described, and interpreted using words and concepts taken from the Old Testament. Without some knowledge of where these have come from, one misses out on a great deal. Think, for example, of John's profound "mash-up" of the Jewish notions of Wisdom and Word to explore the cosmic significance of Christ. Only once we understand the original contexts of these themes and images can we appreciate how they were *reread* in light of Jesus' own "new teaching—with authority!" (Mark 1:27) and the remarkable events surrounding his life, death, and resurrection.

The great saints and theologians of the early Church, some of whom we will meet in the next few chapters, would have agreed wholeheartedly with this approach. Christ came "not to abolish but

43

to fulfil" (Matt 5:17) the Jewish holy books. And "beginning with Moses and the prophets," Jesus himself "interpreted...the things about himself in all the scriptures" (Luke 24:27). Hence Christ's teaching, and the Christian tradition faithful to it (including, above all, the New Testament texts), is not only in full continuity with the Old Testament, but is also the key to making full sense of it. The foundations of this principle are underlined in the New Testament itself:

> Long ago God spoke to our ancestors in many and various ways by the prophets, but in these last days he has spoken to us by a Son, whom he appointed heir of all things, through whom he also created the worlds. He is the reflection of God's glory and the exact imprint of God's very being, and he sustains all things by his powerful word. (Heb 1:1–3)

This basic idea is summed up by Augustine's famous phrase, "In the Old Testament there is a veiling of the New, and in the New Testament there is a revealing of the Old."[7] The Christian understanding of God as Trinity illustrates this perfectly.

You are no doubt familiar with the following analogy, with which Jesus ends the Sermon on the Mount:

> Everyone then who hears these words of mine and acts on them will be like a wise man who built his house on rock. The rain fell, the floods came, and the winds blew and beat on that house, but it did not fall, because it had been founded on rock. (Matt 7:24–25)

The point of the last two chapters was to demonstrate that—and how—the doctrine of the Trinity is one that is solidly "built...on rock": built upon the self-revelation of God, "the spiritual rock" (1 Cor 10:4) and "the rock of our salvation" (Ps 95:1), first in history, and then in the scriptural treasures old and new (cf. Matt 13:52) that testify to it. In the next three chapters we will see how, during the next three hundred or so years, the rains, floods, and winds beat upon this conviction about who God is. "But it did not fall, because it had been founded on rock" (Matt 7:25; cf. 16:18).

Notes

1. Gerald O'Collins, *The Tripersonal God* (London: Continuum, 2004), 11. Many of the examples used throughout this chapter are indebted to O'Collins's much fuller treatment of this topic.

2. St. Melito of Sardis, *On Pascha*, 59–60. Quoted from *On Pascha and Fragments*, ed. and trans. Stuart G. Hall (Oxford: Clarendon Press, 1979), 33.

3. It is often said that *Abba* was a child's word for God in Aramaic, such that Jesus' usage here should be translated into English as "daddy." To the best of my knowledge—and I am, I must admit, no Aramaicist—this idea is no longer widely held. Furthermore, each time the word appears in the New Testament, it is immediately followed by the Greek translation *Pater*, which is the normal Greek term for "Father," rather than for "daddy" or "pops." See John Ashton, "Abba," in *The Anchor Bible Dictionary*, ed. David Noel Freedman, et al., vol. 1: A–C (New York: Doubleday, 1992), 7–8.

4. See, e.g., the differing interpretations of "the oaks of Mamre" episode offered by Justin Martyr in the second century (*Dialogue with Trypho*, 56) and Augustine in the fifth century (*On the Trinity*, II, 19–22).

5. The grander-sounding "tabernacle" comes from the ordinary Latin word for tent, *tabernaculum*.

6. See also the Spirit's descent at Pentecost sounding like "the rush of a violent *wind*" (Acts 2:2).

7. Augustine, *On Catechizing the Uninstructed*, IV, 8. The same idea was taught explicitly at Vatican II: "God, the inspirer and author of both Testaments, wisely arranged that the New Testament be hidden in the Old and the Old be made manifest in the New. For, though Christ established the new covenant in His blood, still the books of the Old Testament with all their parts, caught up into the proclamation of the Gospel, acquire and show forth their full meaning in the New Testament and in turn shed light on it and explain it" (*Dei Verbum* 16).

4

GOD
À LA MODES

The Christian Scriptures, along with the wider Church tradition that nurtured, cherished, and spread them, present us with three basic convictions:

1. There is only one God.
2. The Father, the Son, and the Holy Spirit is each God.
3. The Father, the Son, and the Holy Spirit are not the same.

It cannot be said often enough that this *is* the orthodox doctrine of the Trinity in a nutshell. Over a century before the term was coined (and we'll be discovering when and by whom in this chapter), Christians were thinking and speaking and praying in accordance with these simple principles. In fact, *instincts* is probably a better word here.

The first preachers and teachers knew that each of the above statements, taken individually, was true. What they didn't have, at least not yet, was a coherent way of *saying all three things at once*. It would take the Church centuries to process the strange (Acts 17:20), astounding (Mark 1:22), amazing and perplexing (Acts 2:12) teachings and events of the first century—and indeed, it is still doing so. Many of today's preachers and teachers are, therefore, in good company. We know what we *want* to say about Father, Son, and Holy Spirit, but we often struggle to do so without also saying or implying something we definitely *don't*.

The greatest theological writers of the first two centuries— Paul, John, the author of Hebrews, Justin Martyr—could certainly sympathize. The New Testament authors, for example, often refer to the Father simply as "God" (which, of course, he is), even though they believe that the Son and Spirit are equally God too. The best example comes at the beginning of John: "In the beginning was the Word, and the Word was with God, and the Word was God. He was in the beginning with God" (1:1–2). Since "the Word was God," the second sentence might correctly be written "God [i.e., the Word] was in the beginning with God [i.e., the Father]." However, that would sound as though there are *two* Gods, which John doesn't want to say because he doesn't believe it. Paul does much the same thing in his classic formula: "The grace of the Lord Jesus Christ, the love of God, and the communion of the Holy Spirit be with all of you" (2 Cor 13:13). Naturally, "God" here refers to the Father. Yet elsewhere Paul is perfectly capable of saying Jesus is God (Rom 9:5; cf. Phil 2:6), and—at the very least—implying as much about the Spirit also (1 Cor 1:10–13).

As we saw in chapter 1, talking adequately and meaningfully about God is awkward at the best of times. But it is even harder to do so while remaining faithful to each of our above three "instincts" simultaneously. It is perhaps helpful to think of our three simple sentences as a *trinitarian trilemma*. As we will see in this and the next two chapters, denying (or at least severely downplaying) any one of the three sentences dissolves the problem entirely. The *real* difficulty comes if one refuses to give up any of them, convinced that each one has "been founded on rock" (Matt 7:25). In fact, the great bulk of the often dizzyingly technical theological debates of the first four centuries can be boiled down, and fairly easily understood, in these terms.

▲ ▲ ▲

The modalist controversy, the subject of this chapter, is a case in point. In essence, modalism (sometimes also called Sabellianism, monarchianism, or modalistic monarchianism) can be expressed like so:

1. There is only one God.
2. The Father, the Son, and the Holy Spirit is each God.
3. ~~The Father, the Son, and the Holy Spirit are not the same.~~

Modalist theologians agreed wholeheartedly with the orthodox confession of one God, and were equally happy affirming that the
Father, Son, and Holy Spirit is each God. They did this, however, at
the expense of the idea that Father, Son, and Holy Spirit are distinct.
Hence other theologians, and the consensus of the Church as a
whole, came to view modalism as an opinion (*haeresis*) contrary to
the "correct doctrine" (orthodoxy) of the mainstream Church.

There is a great deal more that could be, and indeed soon will
be, said about modalism. We'll explore the main arguments for
modalism, and what made them seem attractive to certain Christian
thinkers. We'll look at some of the history surrounding the modalist
controversy (since theologizing never happens in a vacuum), and
meet some of the key players on both sides. Significantly, we will see
why the Christian community decided so firmly against the modalists, but also what, along the way, it learned *from* them.

Throughout all of that theological rollercoaster, we will con-
tinually return to our little *trinitarian trilemma*—those three simple,
scriptural sentences that the mainstream Church refused to compromise over—as what the modalist controversy was essentially
about. We'll be doing the same thing in the following chapters, as we
give two other theological wrong turns, subordinationism (or
Arianism) and tritheism, a similar investigation.

▲ ▲ ▲

The modalists were a group of Christian thinkers who came to
prominence in the late second and third centuries. Everything we
know about them comes from people who disagreed with them.
Obviously, that is not ideal from a historical point of view: our
sources have little to gain from presenting their targets in their best
and most charitable light. While we need to be mindful of this, it
shouldn't prevent us getting a sufficient grasp of the modalists'
main ideas.

Writing in the early third century, St. Hippolytus of Rome tells
us that "certain strangers are introducing a strange teaching, disciples as they are of a certain Noetus, who was a Smyrnean by origin,
and lived no great length of time ago."[1] Smyrna, modern-day Izmir
on the west coast of Turkey, was an ancient Christian center, ranked

second only to Ephesus among the "seven churches" in Asia (Rev 1:11). Our other main source, Tertullian, who was writing around the same time, agrees that modalism had recently arrived in Rome "out of Asia."[2] While Hippolytus blames Noetus—pronounced *no-ee-tus*—for this teaching, Tertullian's culprit is someone he nicknames "Praxeas," meaning busybody or meddler. (Tertullian does not hide the fact that, theological disputes aside, there's a fair bit of history between the two of them.[3]) From what we learn about both of them from Hippolytus and Tertullian, Noetus and Praxeas appear to believe very similar things. Some scholars have even suggested that they are one and the same person. Here, we will treat them interchangeably as representatives of the modalist view.

▲ ▲ ▲

Viewed in its best light, modalism is an honest attempt to safeguard the first conviction of our trilemma: "There is only one God." Tertullian describes Praxeas as "the champion of the one Lord."[4] Noetus, we know, was fond of quoting exactly the same kinds of biblical proof texts we used in chapter 2 (e.g., Exod 3:6; Isa 44:6) in order "to establish a single God."[5] So far, both seem very orthodox. Their biggest fear, however, was that this core biblical principle was being ignored—in fact, downright contradicted—by Christian enthusiasm for another core biblical principle: that the Father and Son are both God. If there can only be one, then how can there be two? We have seen the caution with which John and Paul treaded around this problem. Later writers were not always quite so careful. Even so orthodox a theologian as St. Justin Martyr could occasionally slip and speak of Christ as "another God."[6]

To end this confusion, the modalists denied that there is any genuine difference between the Father, the Son and, implicitly, the Holy Spirit.[7] These three names refer, not to different persons, but simply to different ways in which the one God interacts with his creation. The Latin term they used here was *modus* (hence "modalism"), which is where the English word *mode* comes from. Like mode, its basic meaning here is a way or manner of doing something: thus an institution's *modus operandi* is its "way of operating." Computer games give a helpful illustration here. The classic strategy game *Civilization* could be played in seven different modes, ranging from the easiest ("Chieftain") to the most difficult ("Emperor"). In various ways, each one would result in the game playing slightly differently. Regardless, these differences did not add up to seven different games. It was the same game, with seven different ways of interacting with the player; one game, with seven modes. Something similar is the case with the modalists' understanding of who God is. Sometimes God appears in "Father mode," sometimes in "Son mode," and sometimes in "Spirit mode." Each mode looks and *feels* a bit different—God in "Father mode" acts and speaks differently than he does when in "Son mode," and so on— but they're really just the variations of the same basic thing.

Another illustration, one actually used by some of the modalists themselves, might help to make this all a bit clearer. Actors in Greek theatres used to wear large, exaggerated masks. An actor would often play several roles in the same play, and so in each case would put on a different mask. The Greek word used for these masks was *prosōpon* (which is also the Greek word for "face"). Its Latin equivalent was *persona*, from which we get "person." Note that we still sometimes use *persona* in its original way, to refer to a particular character or role a person takes on in certain situations.

Some prominent modalists (including Sabellius the Libyan, a contemporary of Praxeas and Noetus) started referring to the Father and Son as being different *prosōpa*—that is, as different "roles" or "characters" that God plays in his dealings with us. The root metaphor here, of course, is of a single actor simply putting on different masks for different characters. These differences are not purely cosmetic, since the actor performs differently according to which mask he has on, but it's still the same actor underneath each one, *acting* in order to give the illusion of being several different persons.

This is, therefore, how the modalists sought to protect the biblical conviction that "God is one" (Jas 2:14): There is only one God; and Father, Son, and Holy Spirit is each God, because "Father," "Son," and "Holy Spirit" are simply three roles that the one God plays. He is one God, with three personas. This is, one might say, the Sacha Baron Cohen understanding of who God is: there is only one Sacha Baron Cohen, and Ali G, Borat, and Brüno are all Sacha Baron Cohen, because "Ali G," "Borat," and "Brüno" are likewise three personas in Sacha Baron Cohen's repertoire.

▲ ▲ ▲

Don't let that analogy put you off. This view of God is not without its attractions. On the face of it, it is rather a neat way of recon-
ciling the first two horns of our trilemma. As far as the modalists
were concerned, "it is impossible to believe in one God unless...
Father and Son and Holy Spirit are one and the same."[8] Accordingly,
their theology allows us to call the Father, Son, and Holy Spirit
divine, without compromising monotheism. Remember that the
modalists' great fear was that the oneness of God was under attack:
"And so they put it about that by us two or even three gods are
preached, while they, they claim, are worshippers of one God."[9] And
it must also be admitted that certain passages in the Scripture, *if
taken by themselves*, seem to imply something like the modalist view.
It is no surprise that Praxeas and Noetus were both fond of quoting
"The Father and I are one" (John 10:30) and "Whoever has seen me
has seen the Father" (John 14:9).[10] If these were the only things the
Scriptures say about the relationship of Father and Son, then
Praxeas and Noetus might well have a point. The problem, as we've
seen in chapters 2 and 3, is that they're not.

It is worth stressing here just how Scripture-focused the trinitarian debates of the first few centuries actually were. Make no mistake: the early theologians knew their Bibles as well as any contemporary evangelical (indeed far better: the scarcity of manuscripts,
and the absence of indexes, concordances, or online search tools,
meant they had to work from memory). However dry, abstract, technical, or full of jargon these writers can sometimes sound, their primary concern is to interpret the sacred page faithfully—and, of
course, to correct others' failures to do so.

We see this, in abundance, with Hippolytus and Tertullian.
Hippolytus states his method quite clearly:

> Well, let us look at what the Sacred Scriptures proclaim,
> and let us acquire knowledge of what they teach....Not in
> accordance with private choice, nor private interpreta-
> tion, nor by doing violence to the things that God has
> given—but rather let us look at things in the way God

himself resolved to reveal them through the Holy Scriptures.[11]

He criticizes the modalists for selectively quoting from Scripture and for taking phrases out of context: "In fact, whenever they want to get up to their tricks, they hack the Scriptures to pieces. But let [Noetus] quote passages in full, and he will discover the purpose behind what is being said."[12] Tertullian makes the same complaint. He accuses Praxeas of making "a heresy out of the unity"[13] by stressing Scripture's witness to the oneness of God, while pointedly ignoring its testimony to the genuine distinctions between Father, Son, and Spirit. The modalists fixate on two or three proof texts, and try to force all the rest of the evidence to yield to them. This is, Tertullian notes, "the characteristic of all heretics."[14]

▲ ▲ ▲

Remember what we said about the modalists denying the third conviction of our trilemma—that "the Father, the Son, and the Holy Spirit are not the same"? Well, this is precisely Tertullian and Hippolytus's first line of attack. As we saw above, the modalists collapsed the real distinctions within the Godhead: "Father," "Son," and "Holy Spirit" are not three different persons, but merely three roles played by a single actor. Tertullian thinks that this is absurd, and contradicts the plain meaning of Scripture. He mocks the idea—"And so, after all this time, a Father who was born, a Father who suffered...is preached as Jesus Christ"[15]—and elsewhere accuses Praxeas of having "crucified the Father."[16] Tertullian's satire may not, in fact, be so wide of the mark. Apparently quoting one of the modalists themselves, Hippolytus states, "You see, brethren, how rash and reckless a doctrine they introduced in saying quite shamelessly, 'The Father is himself Christ; he is himself the Son; he himself was born, he himself suffered, he himself raised himself up!'"[17] Since the *names* Father, Son, and Spirit don't pick out distinct persons—just different "masks" or "modes"—one might just as easily say that it is the Father who is crucified, or the Son who descends on the disciples at Pentecost, or the Spirit to whom the Lord's Prayer is addressed. They're all the same thing, after all.

However, as we saw in chapters 2 and 3, that doesn't fit at all well with God's self-revelation in history, or in the Scriptures old and new, which testify to, and strive to make sense of, it.

In the first place, the modalist position makes nonsense of those biblical texts which imply at least some kind of plurality *within* the life of God. Tertullian points here, among many other instances, to "Let *us* make humankind in *our* image" (Gen 1:26) and, "See, the man has become like one of *us*" (Gen 3:22). If Praxeas and his ilk are right, Tertullian remarks, then God must be "deceptive or joking in speaking in the plural while being one and alone and singular."[18] If the one God portrays himself as an "us," then he either must be one *in some real sense*, or else he is a liar or a joker. Tertullian is in no doubt as to which option he is betting on.

Time and again, Tertullian insists one should accept Scripture's "clearly defined and simple statements"[19] on this point at face value. And the simple fact is that the Bible depicts Father, Son, and Holy Spirit as being, in some real way, distinct. As previously noted, this is clearest when we see one person of the Trinity talking either to, or about, one or more of the others. Jesus praying to his Father in heaven (Mark 14:36), or the Father telling him, "You are my Son, the Beloved" (Mark 1:11), or the Spirit being sent from the Father by the Son to testify on his behalf (John 15:26)...unless these are to be understood as elaborate pieces of ventriloquism, then they "establish each person as being himself and none other."[20]

▲ ▲ ▲

Tertullian's and Hippolytus's critiques of the modalist position go deeper still. There is no room here to recount all their various arguments (each of them, incidentally, supported by reams of scriptural evidence). However, let us examine just two more.

According to the modalists, the Father and the Son are one and the same person (Sabellius used to speak of the "Sonfather"— *Huiopater* in Greek—to emphasize this idea). "He himself, they say, made himself his own son."[21] But this is, as Tertullian rightly recognized, illogical and absurd. *Father* and *Son* are special kinds of titles. They imply a certain form of relationship between two (or more) who are distinct:

A father must have a son so as to be father, and a son must have a father so as to be a son. For to have is one thing, to be is another: for example, to be a husband I must have a wife, I shall not be my own wife. So also, that I may be a father I have a son, I shall not be my own son: and that I may be a father I have son, I shall not be my own son.[22]

Naturally, it is perfectly possible for a single person to be both a father and a son—indeed, I am just such a person. But I am a father because there are *others* (my children), with whom I am in a specific kind of relationship. And I am a son because there are *others* (my parents), with whom I am in another specific kind of relationship. The very words themselves require the existence of distinct persons. But that is precisely what Praxeas and Noetus deny of the Godhead. Tertullian is right. In arguing that God must be "Father-and-Son," without distinguishing between persons, the modalists end up with a God who is, and can only be, neither Father nor Son.

This brings us nicely to "The Father and I are one" (John 10:30), a phrase understandably dear to the hearts of Praxeas and Noetus. As is clear from the above arguments, Father and Son can't "be one" in the same sense that, say, Johnny Cash and the Man in Black are. However, our champions of orthodoxy go further, both making similar grammatical arguments. Hippolytus and Tertullian each points out that Jesus uses a *plural* verb here. Quoting the former: "He did not say, 'I and the Father *am* one,' but '*are* one.' 'We are' is not said with reference to one, but with reference to two."[23] To be fair to their opponents, this level of technical detail, which Tertullian characteristically takes even further,[24] looks a little like hairsplitting. In English, at least, we wouldn't insist on saying "Johnny Cash and the Man in Black *is* one" to denote their identity. Nevertheless, as we have seen, the orthodox case rests on far more solid arguments than this particular one, although it's worth mentioning, simply to underline the level of scriptural detail being entered into in these trinitarian debates. These are not vague appeals to scriptural themes or ideas: battles are being fought over whether one verb in the Gospels is plural or singular. It cannot be said often enough: Christianity developed and defended its understanding of God as Trinity not despite, but demonstrably because of and out of, the biblical witness. As Hippolytus remarks, "The whole of the Scriptures are a proclamation about this."[25]

▲ ▲ ▲

Tertullian's and Hippolytus's contributions to the Church's gradual sharpening of its trinitarian instincts were not, however, wholly negative. And nor, for that matter, were those of the modalists.

It is worth remembering that the modalist position was a reaction to widespread confusion about *how* Father, Son, and Holy Spirit could each be God, and an accompanying fear that the biblical conviction that "the Lord is one" (Deut 6:4, NIV) was being undermined by careless talk of Christ as "another God" besides the Father. We have seen how even the finest theologians of the first two centuries sometimes struggled to say everything they wanted to, without also saying (or implying) things that they definitely didn't. The modalists brought this issue into the open, and forced other Christians to think harder about what exactly they needed to say about God, and how to go about it. If the mainstream Church refused to compromise on any item in its trinitarian trilemma, then it would need to find an adequate language to hold true to all three simple statements without descending into nonsense.

That is precisely what Tertullian, in particular, started to do. He began by combining the Latin words *trias* (three) and *unitas* (unity) to make up *trinitas*.[26] Transposed into English, this gives us *Trinity*— a bespoke word, tailored to express both threeness and oneness. As if that coinage wasn't enough, he was also one of the first to start talking about this Trinity as comprising three distinct *personae* or "persons" (i.e., Father, Son, and Holy Spirit), who are nonetheless one *substantia* or "substance" (i.e., their shared divinity). As we will see in chapter 6, this kind of language for talking about the Trinity would prove very influential. However, recall that *persona*, along with its Greek equivalent *prosōpon*, was the very term that the heretic modalists also used (albeit somewhat differently) to describe Father, Son, and Spirit. Tertullian took the word, found it useful, and reshaped its meaning for orthodox ends. As we shall see in the next two chapters, this will be a persistent theme in the Church's development of its trinitarian theology. Still, credit where credit is due. In the words of Joseph Ratzinger,

All the same, it need not be denied that the efforts of [the modalists] resulted in noteworthy progress towards a correct conception of God; after all, the language of Christianity adopted the terminology which they developed and in the confession of faith in the three persons in God it is still at work today.[27]

▲ ▲ ▲

Tertullian and Hippolytus were both writing in the first decades of the third century. It would be fanciful to suggest that, chastened by their superior arguments, all the modalists repented of their views, issued apologetic prayers to each member of the Blessed Trinity *individually*, and the Church was never again troubled by deniers of the scriptural conviction that "Father, Son, and Holy Spirit are not the same." Nevertheless, over time, the types of arguments advanced by Hippolytus and Tertullian ultimately won the day. History records some later modalists, cropping up here and there, throughout the third century. Significantly, these include the heretical Antiochene bishop, Paul of Samosata, who enjoyed using the term *homoousios* ("same-substance") to describe the identity of Father and Son, for which, even more significantly, he and his followers were condemned by a much wider consensus of bishops in the 260s.

By and large, however, modalism became best known not as in any sense a "live option" for Christians trying to understand who God is, but rather as one of the great textbook examples of heresy: a cautionary tale of how *not* to do trinitarian theology. *Everybody* knew that Sabellianism, as it was near-universally known in the early Church, was a bad thing, even if they were not necessarily sure what Sabellianism actually entailed.

In terms of the Church's gradual working out of who their God had revealed himself to be, the modalist controversy marked a significant moment. One third of the trinitarian trilemma had been subject to attack (under the guise of championing the other two).

However, aided by such colorful characters as Tertullian and Hippolytus (neither of whose personal histories are exactly uncheckered), the Church had refused to budge. The Scriptures were not simply to be "hack[ed]... to pieces,"[28] no matter how awkward doing full justice to them might sometimes feel. And in standing firm, the early Church began to gather and hone the words and concepts it would need to make the task a little less awkward in the future.

Notes

1. Hippolytus, *Against Noetus*, 1. This text is often referred to by its Latin name, *Contra Noetum* (which simply means "Against Noetus"). Translations of *Against Noetus* are easily available online, and the paragraph numbers used here should be standard across different versions. The exact translation I am quoting, however, is this one: Hippolytus of Rome, *Contra Noetum*, ed. and trans. Robert Butterworth (London: Heythrop Monographs, 1977), 42–93.

2. *Against Praxeas*, 1. Pretty much everything said in the previous endnote applies here too. The exact translation of Tertullian's *Adversus Praxean* (its Latin title) I am quoting here is taken from Alexander Roberts and James Donaldson, eds., *Ante-Nicene Fathers*, vol. 3: *Latin Christianity: Its Founder, Tertullian; I. Apologetic; II. Anti-Marcion; III. Ethical* (Edinburgh: T. & T. Clark, [1885] 1996), 597–627.

3. Tertullian was a supporter of the "New Prophecy" or Montanism, founded in the late second century by a Turkish prophet, Montanus, along with two prophetesses, Priscilla and Maximilla. This ascetical and charismatic movement spread quickly, and gained significant numbers of followers in Rome and North Africa. For various moral, liturgical, and doctrinal reasons—later writers, at least, accused Montanus of claiming to be the Paraclete or Holy Spirit—the New Prophecy was deemed unorthodox, and Montanist groups broke away from the mainstream Church. (For more on this topic, see Christine Trevett, "Montanism," in *The Early Christian World*, ed. Philip F. Esler, vol. 2 [New York: Routledge, 2000], 929–51.)

On *this* matter, Praxeas (whatever his other faults) was on the right side. It seems he was partly responsible for the New Prophecy's condemnation by the Bishop of Rome, prompting Tertullian (whatever his other virtues) to include the fact he "drove out prophecy" and "put to flight the paraclete" to add to his other pieces of "the Devil's business" (*Against Praxeas*, 1). Whether Tertullian himself actually left, or was kicked out of, the Church is not fully clear.

It is worth remembering that even the "good guys"—as Tertullian certainly is on the topic of the Trinity—are not always straightforwardly so. The other great hero of this chapter, the saint and martyr, Hippolytus, spent a good chunk of his life as an antipope (i.e., as a false bishop of Rome).

4. Tertullian, *Against Praxeas*, 1.

5. Hippolytus, *Against Noetus*, 2.

6. Justin Martyr, *Dialogue with Trypho*, 56. Quoted from Alexander Roberts and James Donaldson, eds., *Ante-Nicene Fathers*, vol. 1: *The Apostolic Fathers, Justin Martyr, Irenaeus* (Edinburgh: T. & T. Clark, [1885] 1996), 194–270.

7. Though the focus of these debates was the relationship of the Father and the Son, the points raised—as Tertullian makes plain—relate just as much to the Spirit as well. Throughout this chapter, we will often include the Spirit in our discussion, even when the original sources are *directly* talking only about the Father and the Son.

8. Tertullian, *Against Praxeas*, 2.

9. Ibid., 3.

10. See Tertullian, *Against Praxeas*, 20; Hippolytus, *Against Noetus*, 7.

11. Hippolytus, *Against Noetus*, 9.

12. Ibid., 4.

13. Tertullian, *Against Praxeas*, 1.

14. Ibid., 20.

15. Ibid., 9.

16. Ibid., 1.

17. Hippolytus, *Against Noetus*, 3.

18. Tertullian, *Against Praxeas*, 12.

19. Ibid., 13.

20. Ibid., 11.

21. Ibid., 10.
22. Ibid.
23. Hippolytus, *Against Noetus*, 7.
24. See Tertullian, *Against Praxeas*, 22.
25. Hippolytus, *Against Noetus*, 14.
26. Tertullian, *Against Praxeas*, 2.
27. Joseph Ratzinger, *Introduction to Christianity* (London: Search Press, 1971), 118.
28. Hippolytus, *Against Noetus*, 4.

5

TRUE GOD
FROM TRUE GOD

The triumph of the antimodalists is proven, if a bit ironically, by the Arian crisis of the following century. This all began in the bustling Egyptian port of Alexandria around the year 318. According to the fifth-century historian Socrates Scholasticus, the bishop Alexander preached a homily on the Trinity. A priest named Arius, "imagining that the bishop was subtly teaching the same view...as Sabellius the Libyan," began to denounce him as a heretic, and the matter very swiftly escalated.[1] By this time, the serious faults in the modalist approach were fully recognized; Tertullian and Hippolytus had well and truly won the day. Yet in his overeagerness to hunt out heresies (since Alexander and his supporters really *weren't* modalists at all), Arius soon revealed the deep and heretical flaws in his own, and many others', theology. "Thus from a little spark a large fire was kindled"[2]— indeed, an inferno that required the Church's first two ecumenical Councils (at Nicaea in 325, and Constantinople in 381) in order to douse it.

The previous century's arguments centered on the third horn of our trilemma (i.e., whether or not Father, Son, and Holy Spirit are all the same). Now it was time for the second to undergo lengthy and searching scrutiny. In the simplest terms, Arius and his allies insisted that the Son could not *really* be God. Strictly speaking, things are a little more complicated than that: they were happy to *call* him God, but they were clear that he could not possibly *be* God in the full and true sense that the Father is God. As was also the case with the modalist dispute, the Holy Spirit isn't often the direct focus of attention here. Yet as before, most of the same issues about the

Son apply, at least implicitly, to the Spirit also. Expressed in the terms of our trilemma, therefore, the Arian position looks like this:

1. There is only one God.
2. ~~The Father, the Son, and the Holy Spirit is each God.~~
3. The Father, the Son, and the Holy Spirit are not the same.

Arianism is hence the second false solution to our Scripture-derived trilemma. By eliminating—or at least, severely downplaying—statement 2, there is no difficulty in holding statements 1 (the oneness of God) and 3 (the distinctness of Father, Son, and Holy Spirit) together. For Arius, the three persons of the Trinity are certainly not the same (3), since only the Father is the one, true God (1). The Son, though special, is infinitely inferior to the Father ~~(2)~~. For this reason, Arianism is often known as *subordinationism*. The Son is, by his very nature, subordinate—that is, lower or inferior—to the Father. The same applies to the Spirit too, of course.

▲ ▲ ▲

To understand Arius, we must first understand what he thought he was opposing. Helpfully, Arius's chief objections to his bishop's preaching have been preserved in one of his letters. He complains that Alexander is teaching that the Son has always existed ("Always God, always Son"; "At the same time Father, at the same time Son"), and that there never was a moment before the Father *was* a father ("Neither in thought nor in some moment of time does God proceed the Son"). What's worse, Alexander even claims that "the Son is from God himself."[3]

Arius's problems might not be immediately obvious. Essentially, what Alexander is trying to assert with such statements—and Arius is seeking to condemn by quoting them—is the idea that the Son is really and truly God, just as much as the Father is. Thus the Father and Son are coeternal, and the Son was timelessly born (or "begotten") out of the Father's very nature or substance. Admittedly, Alexander confuses things here by referring to the Father simply as "God," even when asserting that the Son is truly God as well. However, as we saw in the last chapter, this is exactly what John's Gospel does too. The parallel is surely not coincidental,

62

since John's Prologue is precisely an affirmation of God the Son's begottenness from, and coeternality with, God the Father ("In the beginning was the Word, and the Word was with God, and the Word was God," "God the only Son," etc.). In fact, it is tempting to suppose that Alexander's original sermon was an exposition of John 1, though we have no way of knowing for sure.

Why Arius is so horrified by Alexander's alleged "impieties"[4] becomes clear from his own counterviews. These too have survived in Arius's own words, from his letters and short quotations from the *Thalia*, a poetic popularization of his ideas, preserved by his critic St. Athanasius (who describes it as "flippant," having an "effeminate manner and melody," and containing "jokes...which are full of impiety and to be avoided"[5]).

▲ ▲ ▲

Viewed charitably, Arius's theology is an attempt to affirm the distinction between Father and Son (versus modalism), coupled with a sophisticated exaltation of divine otherness. As he writes to Alexander,

> We know one God—alone unbegotten, alone everlasting, alone without beginning, alone true, alone possessing immortality, alone wise, alone good, alone master, judge of all, manager, director, immutable and unchangeable, just and good, God of Law, Prophets, and New Testament.[6]

Taken by itself, that might just about sound orthodox enough. Arius is keen to list all the heresies (including, of course, that of Sabellius) to which he *doesn't* subscribe.[7] However, it is essential to realize that Arius applies the above doxology exclusively to the Father. But if *only* the Father is "everlasting," "without beginning," "possessing immortality" and the rest, then who or what is the Son?

The shortest and most important answer to that question is this: a creature. A glorious and powerful creature, to be sure, the first and greatest part of creation (cf. Col 1:15)—but a created thing nonetheless. The Son is said to have been "created by the will of God before time and ages,"[8] and summoned into existence "from nothing":[9] "The Son, begotten by the Father, created and founded before the ages, was not before he was begotten....For he is not everlasting or co-everlasting or unbegotten with the Father."[10] Arius's view of the Son is perhaps best summed up by the phrase he himself uses while defending himself to Alexander: "[a] perfect creature of God, but not as one of the [other] creatures."[11]

▲ ▲ ▲

Arius's Son is a sort of superangel. He is a created being, and thus infinitely inferior to the Creator. Yet he is also a supernatural one, endowed with "life, being, and glories from the Father as the Father has shared them with him."[12] He is thus vastly superior to every other created thing, including us. This statement results in one of the strangest (and most misleading) aspects of Arius's theology: the use of the title *God* for a being that he and his followers are adamant *isn't*.

In one of his letters, for example, Arius describes the Son as being "full of grace and truth, God, only-begotten, unchangeable."[13] But how can this be, if the Son is only a creature? It is here that Arius introduces a subtle distinction. In the *Thalia* he explains, "Even if he is declared God, he is not true God. By sharing grace, he is declared God only in name."[14] The Son is not, therefore, *really* God. Only the Father is true God, but the Son can be called *God* as a kind of honorary, courtesy title.

Admittedly, this muddies the waters a little vis-à-vis our trilemma. For the Arians can say that they *do* affirm that the Father and Son, at least, is each God. However, what they mean by calling the Son *God* is something radically different from how the word is normally used—and indeed, how they themselves use it of the Father. This difference is underlined by Arius's insistence that "the Father is other than the Son in substance [*ousia*],"[15] and that "the substances [*ousiae*] of the Father, Son, and Holy Spirit are divided in nature, estranged, detached, alien, and nonsharers in one another."[16] *Ousia* is a Greek philosophical term, meaning substance, essence, or nature: you and I, for example, both share the *ousia* of humanness. To put it a bit loosely, what Arius is saying here is that Father, Son, and Holy Spirit are totally different kinds of things. To my mind—you may of course disagree—this doesn't even come close to doing full justice to our principle that "Father, Son, and Holy Spirit is each God." This is a point to which we shall return. However, note that only a slight modification to our original sentence really would rule out any Arian work-around: "2. Father, Son, and Holy Spirit is each *truly* God."

To summarize: perhaps a helpful way of picturing all this is to think of the 1940 film *Pinocchio*. Pinocchio is a walking, talking, living puppet fashioned by Geppetto in lieu of a "real boy" to love as his son. Although created from wood like every other thing the elderly carpenter has produced, Pinocchio possesses a range of remarkable supernatural powers. He is, if you like, a perfect creation of Geppetto's, but not as one of his other creations. While Pinocchio shares several characteristics with human children—one might even *call* him a boy—he is not himself a *real* boy. By the same token, Geppetto might have adopted him as his son, call him his son, and love him as his son. But Pinocchio is not really a son, Geppetto's or otherwise. And Geppetto is not really a father, Pinocchio's or otherwise. Pinocchio was made, not begotten or born, and he does not have the same *ousia* as Geppetto: humans and wooden puppets, even very special ones, are divided in nature. While I'm not entirely sure that Disney *intended* to produce a feature-length satire of Arian Christology, that's pretty much what they achieved.[17]

▲ ▲ ▲

Had this simply been a dispute between a priest and his bishop, nobody would still be reading about Arius seventeen hundred years later. It wasn't. We have spoken extensively of Arius, and of something called "Arianism," but the man himself and his allies would have found this disturbing. So far as they were concerned, this was simply Christianity: "Our faith, from our ancestors."[18] This explains why the controversy escalated so swiftly, and how Arius could soon count as compatriots a number of bishops. While Arius's claim to have enlisted nearly "all the bishops throughout the East"[19] should be taken with a handful of salt, among his comrades were the famous historian Eusebius of Caesarea, and the emperor's close confidant, Eusebius of Nicomedia. These were neither stupid nor politically unsavvy; they certainly did not see themselves as mere groupies of an upstart presbyter. Arius could also point to local precedents. Decades earlier, the celebrated (though later condemned) Alexandrian theologian Origen had also differentiated between "God" and "true God," and insisted that the Son and the Spirit were created.[20] The fundamental issues at stake between Alexander and Arius therefore were both widespread and deepseated. It was a controversy not just waiting, but *needing*, to happen.

Regardless, a bitter ecclesiastical civil war was the last thing anybody needed. Christianity had been decriminalized in the Roman Empire less than a decade ago. The empire itself was, slowly, emerging from a lengthy period of violent discord. The new Emperor Constantine, who credited the God of the Christians for his own run of good luck, was thus particularly displeased by this new source of trouble. A letter to both Alexander and Arius, sent in late 324, expresses his disappointment that "the whole of Africa was pervaded by an intolerable spirit of mad folly."[21] Despite his own court bishop, Eusebius of Nicomedia, being heavily involved in this "mad folly," Constantine betrays no real understanding of the disagreement and its import. He even goes so far as to dismiss the issues as "some trifling and foolish verbal difference."[22]

There is a great deal of historical detail that we must skip over here. This is not, after all, primarily intended as a work of church history. *The* key event, though, and one of the defining moments in the history of Christianity, happens in the year 325: the Church's first universal council, held at Nicaea (now the Turkish lake resort of İznik).

▲ ▲ ▲

The idea of gathering Church leaders to settle doctrinal and pastoral disagreements is a thoroughly biblical one. The so-called Council of Jerusalem in Acts 15, concerning the expectations upon Gentile converts, is the model here: "The apostles and elders met together to consider the matter" (15:6), provoking "much debate" (15:7). Local councils or synods of all the bishops from a particular region were an established feature of church life by the early fourth century. Mostly, these were routine affairs discussing matters of administration, discipline, and policy (the regular plenary meetings of today's national bishops' conferences perhaps give a flavor). Yet every so often something "big" would emerge, and the bishops of the affected areas would meet to deliberate and decide.

Nicaea was different, insofar as all the bishops of the "inhabited world" (*oikumenē*, hence "ecumenical" council) were invited to attend. In practice, only around 250 to 318—estimates vary—did so. Very few western bishops journeyed to the far east of the empire to adjudicate upon matters of which they likely had little detailed knowledge. (Remember that the Arian controversy was conducted almost exclusively in Greek, whereas the western half of the empire—Rome included—was mainly Latin-speaking.) Those gathered in May 325 were, however, sufficiently representative—every Roman province (except Britain) had at least one delegate, and a Spanish bishop, Ossius of Cordoba, chaired the meeting—to signal "the consent of the whole church" (Acts 15:22).

The Council of Nicaea met for the best part of two months. How the discussion went is a matter of conjecture. Not in doubt, though, is the fact that the assembled bishops resoundingly rejected the Arian position. To prove this, they produced a startlingly polemical statement of orthodoxy, full of phrases that no self-respecting Arian could put his name to in good conscience. (Though that didn't stop a good number of them, evidently mindful of which way the wind was blowing, from signing up regardless—the two bishops Eusebius included.[23]) This statement is, of course, what we now know as the Nicene Creed...well, *almost*. Technically, the creed that is now recited on Sundays throughout the world is an expanded version of the original, courtesy of the Council of Constantinople in 381—but we'll get to that later.

▲ ▲ ▲

One cannot fully appreciate the Creed without grasping at least some of its background; all the more reason, I might add, for making the Church's gradual digestion of the Trinity's self-revelation in history better known among the people of God. So knowing what we now know, let's look at it afresh. Below is the original text from Nicaea, rendered into English:

We believe in one God, the Father almighty, maker of all things visible and invisible.

We believe in one Lord Jesus Christ, the Son of God, **begotten from the Father as only-begotten (that is to say, from the substance [*ousia*] of the Father), God from God**, light from light, **true God from true God**, **begotten not made, consubstantial [*homoousios*] with the Father**, through whom all things were made, the things in heaven and the things on earth. For us men and for our salvation, he came down, and was incarnated and made man. He suffered, rose on the third day, ascended into heaven, and is coming to judge the living and dead.

And in the Holy Spirit.

Ignore the bold sections for a moment, and look first at the overall, oddly uneven structure. It isn't so strange, however, once you know the Arian controversy centered on the nature and status of the Son, and that the Spirit was, at least to begin with, rarely discussed directly. That explains why the Son gets a whole paragraph, compared to the Father's sentence, and the Holy Spirit's mere five words.

Now, look at the bold phrases, each one calculated to rule out anything approaching Arius's views. Let's briefly consider each in turn:

"Begotten from the Father...(that is to say, from the substance [*ousia*] of the Father)": The Son is truly born from out of the Father's very nature. Arius, by contrast, had criticized Alexander for saying the "the Son is from God himself."[24]

"God from God...true God from true God": The Council has no truck with Arius's linguistic gerrymandering, distinguishing "God" from "true God." "God from God" is a traditional phrase found in earlier creeds, but can just about be subjected to an Arian interpretation. "True God from true God," however, flatly contradicts Arius's contention that "the Word is not true God."[25]

"Begotten not made": Though Arius believed the Son to be created from nothing, he was happy enough to call him "begotten" in a metaphorical sense. The Arians accordingly used *begotten* and *made/created* more or less interchangeably, as in the claim, "He begot him not in appearance but in truth...[a] perfect creature of God."[26]

The council fathers here drive a wedge between the two concepts. Among other reasons, the idea that the Son is "begotten" is thoroughly scriptural (e.g., John 3:16; 1 John 4:9); the idea that he was "made," like every other creature, most certainly isn't.

"**Consubstantial [*homoousios*] with the Father**": Nicaea's Arius-baiting now reaches its summit. According to a much later legend, at one point in the council's proceedings, Arius was punched in the face by St. Nicholas of Myra, a Turkish bishop now better known as Santa Claus. True or not, the Creed's inclusion of the Greek word *homoousios* [*hommo-oo-see-oss*] is at least a theological slap in the face. *Homo-* means "the same" (as in homosexual or homogenized). *-Ousios*, as we have already seen, means nature, essence, or substance (which is from where, via Latin, we get our word *consubstantial*). To say that the Son is *homoousios* with the Father, then, is to say that they share the same fundamental nature—that is to say, that the Son is as fully God as the Father is. Such a claim is obviously unacceptable to Arius. Indeed, he specifically denies it in the *Thalia*, writing that the Son "is not equal to God, nor yet is of the same substance (*homoousios*)."[27] The council's deliberate use of the term was doubly provocative, since it had previously been used (albeit in a different sense) by some of the third-century modalists. (This is yet another example of the phenomenon noted by Ratzinger in chapter 4: heretical language being borrowed, reconditioned, and reemployed for orthodox ends.) In the sense intended by Nicaea, the word *homoousios* perfectly captures the heart of the Church's proclamation of the Son as "the Messiah, who is over all, God blessed for ever" (Rom 9:5). No doubt Arius, though, just saw it as confirmation of what he had wrongly been arguing all along: that Alexander and his allies were Sabellians.

These phrases are not the *only* anti-Arian aspects of the Creed. Arius was likely none too keen on "light from light" either, for example.[28] What's more, the original version contains a coda really ramming the point home (as if it hadn't already!):

And those who say "there was once when he was not" or "he was not before he was begotten" or "he came into existence from nothing" or who affirm that the Son of God is of another *hypostasis* or substance (*ousia*), or a creature, or mutable or subject to change, such ones the catholic and apostolic Church pronounces accursed and separated from the Church.[29]

One could hardly wish for a more robust assertion of the Son's full divinity—and defence against a potent assault on the second horn of our trilemma.

▲ ▲ ▲

Although the Council of Nicaea was undoubtedly the key landmark in the Arian controversy, it was very far from signaling the end of it. True, "the ecumenical synod, not enduring Arius' impiety, cast Arius out of the Church...and anathematized him."[30] (He later negotiated a return to the Church, but reportedly died before this actually happened. This occasioned some not very edifying gloating on the part of some otherwise saintly Church fathers.) As remarked upon above, however, the collection of theological views that we now know as "Arianism," were spread more widely and deeply than that nickname would imply. The same or similar ideas stubbornly persisted, so the subordinationist controversy rumbled on for another good half decade. We'll briefly catch up on Nicaea's aftermath at the end of this chapter. Now we might pause to consider just *why* the council reacted so forcefully to the ideas Arius and many others upheld. In hindsight, the protractedness of the Arian affair—dragging on for the best (or perhaps worst) part of the fourth century—was theologically providential. It meant that the issues in question, and the arguments for and against, were given a thorough going over by all sides. Weighing in were some of the finest theological minds of that or any other generation. Chief among them are two names we've already met in passing: St. Athanasius of Alexandria, who attended Nicaea as a deacon and later succeeded Alexander as bishop, and St. Gregory of Nazianzus, known to later centuries as "the Theologian," and one of a celebrated trio of Turkish bishop-saints known as the Cappadocian fathers. (We'll be meeting the others, the brothers Basil the Great and Gregory of Nyssa, in this and the next chapter.)

Evidently, the universal Church's primary objection to Arianism—as expressed by the teaching authority of its first general

Council—was, in Alexander's words, "that they deny the divinity of our Saviour."[31] The biblical basis of the Church's belief that Christ was God has already been given in chapter 2. To this general body of evidence, a number of subarguments addressing specific Arian claims were added. Take, for example, Alexander's objection to the suggestion that the Son was created out of nothing. Appealing to John 1:3, he pointedly asks, "If 'all things came into existence through him,' how is it that he who gave being to the ones who came into existence once was not?"[32] The overriding sticking point with Arianism, however, was simply this: Scripture and Tradition testify that Christ was really, truly "God...with us" (Matt 1:23), and so no amount of watering down could be permitted. This demanded nothing less than the full confession that, in Gregory's words, the Son is "a God who is for us true and equal in honor."[33] By contrast, Arius's "ambiguous and interpolated 'god'"[34]—a supercreature we may *call* God even though he isn't—just won't do. In fact, as Athanasius points out, it is nothing short of idolatry: "They, when they say that the Son of the Father, the Word of God, is a created being, differ in nought from the heathen, since they worship that which is created, rather than God the creator."[35]

Not explicitly addressed by Nicaea, however, is *why* the Son must be "true God, *homoousios* with the true Father."[36] Scriptural arguments aside, wouldn't an Arian superangel or cosmic Pinocchio do the job just as well? The answer to that question, which developed in detail only after Nicaea, is a flat no. The reason for this ultimately boils down to the following: "God's love was revealed among us in this way: God sent his only Son into the world so that we might live through him" (1 John 4:9).

▲ ▲ ▲

Athanasius and Gregory both emphasize the centrality of *salvation* to our understanding of the Trinity. Trinitarian speculation is not some remote, abstract puzzle, a form of "celestial Sudoku."[37] It gets to the very heart of Christian hope. If the Son is not truly God—if it were a mere creature who was made man, suffered, died, and rose again—then it has all been in vain.

For Athanasius, this follows directly from a properly scriptural vision of quite what salvation entails. The resurrected Christ, as "first-born from the dead" (Col 1:18), is indeed the promise of our bodily resurrection. Yet that is only the half of it. The glory of his risen body, and his ascension into heaven, are likewise "the first fruits" (1 Cor 15:20) of our own glory. In the incarnate Lord, human nature is *already* exalted in the highest heaven (cf. Heb 6:19–20; 9:24). He is the "forerunner on our behalf" (Heb 6:20), offering us the possibility of becoming "participants of the divine nature" (2 Pet 1:4).

> Because of our relationship to his body, even we became God's temple, and now we are made sons of God, so that already the Lord is worshiped in us, and those who see "announce" as the apostle said that "truly God is in them" (1 Corinthians 14:25). John says in the Gospel, "But as many as received him, he gave them power to become children of God" (John 1:12)....If the Lord had not become man, we would not, having been redeemed from sins, rise from the dead, but we would remain dead beneath the earth. We would not be exalted in heaven, but we would lie in Hades.[38]

In truly becoming the true man Jesus of Nazareth, the true God has assumed human nature. This has radical implications for us all. Famously, Athanasius, in common with many of the Church fathers, does not shy away from expressing this in startling terms: "He deified that which he put on, and more, he offered this to the human race."[39] Gregory is blunter still, noting that the incarnation's purpose was "so that I might become God as he became man."[40]

While certainly heady, there is great deal more that could be said on this topic (and perhaps should be to avoid misinterpretation—though that will have to wait for another book). For our purposes, it should be clear enough that the Arians' Son, "God" in name only, cannot possibly be up to such a task. Only God—*the real one*—can save us. Accept no subordinates.

▲ ▲ ▲

In 381, a second ecumenical council was convened at Constantinople, the imperial city. Like Nicaea, its intention was finally to draw a line under the Arian controversy. Unlike Nicaea, it more or less succeeded.[41] Arguably, the sheer weight of the questions thrown up by Arius—who the Son is, and who he *must be* in order to bring "the hope of eternal life that God, who never lies, promised before the ages began" (Tit 1:2)—needed properly thrashing out. The solutions insisted upon by Nicaea, correct though they were, came too early into this process to be roundly accepted. Only when the ground had been thoroughly prepared by the labors of Athanasius, Gregory, and others could the seeds planted by Nicaea fully "bear...fruit and yield" (Matt 13:23). In retrospect, these are glorious and easily romanticized decades in the history of orthodoxy. Yet, as ever, they did not seem so at the time. Athanasius was exiled from Alexandria no less than five times between the two councils, and once spent four months hiding out in his own father's tomb. In a famous comment on the turmoil following Nicaea, St. Basil the Great despairingly asked, "What storm at sea was ever so fierce and wild as this tempest of the Churches?...And who could make a complete list of all the wrecks?"[42]

Yet the storms abated, and after 381 Athanasius was never forcibly removed from his diocese again. The Council of Constantinople reasserted the teaching of Nicaea. It also updated it to reflect some more recent theological disputes. For example, the divinity of the Holy Spirit had been questioned by a group known, catchily enough, as the "Spirit-fighters" (*pneumatamachoi*). This too was a matter needing to come out into the open. As we have noted, the Spirit is mentioned only infrequently in the modalist and early Arian debates. Nicaea says simply, "We believe...in the Holy Spirit." This oversight was soon rectified, however, with Athanasius, Gregory, and Basil again leading the charge to affirm the full divinity of the Spirit too: "What, then? Is the Spirit God? Certainly. Is he consubstantial (*homoousios*)? Yes, if he is God."[43]

Constantinople therefore produced what one might call the "Director's Cut" of the Nicene Creed. This revised and expanded version includes the following "bonus scenes":

...and in the Holy Spirit, the Lord, the giver of life, who proceeds from the Father, who with the Father and the

Son is adored and glorified, who has spoken through the prophets.

And in one holy, catholic, and apostolic Church. We confess one baptism for the forgiveness of sins, and we look forward to the resurrection of the dead and the life of the world to come. Amen.

Essentially, this is what—with just one, tiny further addition (see chapter 7)—is now known by Catholics as the Nicene Creed today.

▲ ▲ ▲

Arianism has some claim to being the greatest heresy in the history of Christianity. It strikes right at the heart of the ancient Christian proclamation of "Jesus Christ, Son of God, Savior." It forced the Church to clarify, once and for all, some lingering grey areas concerning the Son and Spirit's status and their relationship to the Father. It stimulated the idea of ecumenical councils as a means of exercising the universal Church's teaching authority promised by Christ (Matt 16:17–19; John 14:26; 16:13), and it drove out into the open a fact that was largely only implicit in earlier trinitarian theology: that a correct understanding of the divine triunity isn't merely a theological party game. Rather, it is essential for making sense of our "hope of glory" (Col 1:27).

We have now seen two separate attempts to dissolve away the trinitarian trilemma, by denying one of its core pillars. The second- and third-century modalist controversy subjected our third statement ("Father, Son, and Holy Spirit are not the same") to searching scrutiny. In the fourth century, the Arian controversy did the honors regarding our second statement ("Father, Son, and Holy Spirit is each God"). Both times we have seen the wider Church tradition, and the scriptural witness inspiring it, emerge victorious. Along the way, the universal Church acquired (or stole!) certain words and concepts—*trinity, person, nature, consubstantial*—sometimes subtly changing their meaning in the process. Gradually, Christianity was finding a more-or-less satisfactory way of *saying all three things at once*. In defending the remaining third of the trilemma ("There is only God"), it finally hit upon it. Let us see how.

74

Notes

1. Socrates Scholasticus, *The Ecclesiastical History*, 5. The translation used here may be found in Philip Schaff and Henry Wace, eds., *Nicene and Post-Nicene Fathers*, series 2, vol. 2: *Socrates, Sozomenus; Church Histories* (Peabody, MA: Hendrickson, [1890] 1994), 1–178.

2. Ibid., 6.

3. Arius, *Letter to Eusebius of Nicomedia*, 2 (Rusch, 29). Unless otherwise stated, all the primary sources quoted in this chapter are taken from the translations included in William G. Rusch, ed. and trans., *The Trinitarian Controversy* (Philadelphia: Fortress Press, 1980). Page references to this translation will be given in parantheses.

4. Ibid., 4 (Rusch, 29).

5. Athanasius, *Orations against the Arians*, I, 5 (Rusch, 66).

6. Arius, *Letter to Alexander of Alexandria*, 2 (Rusch, 31).

7. Ibid.

8. Ibid., 3 (Rusch, 32).

9. Arius, *Letter to Eusebius of Nicomedia*, 5 (Rusch, 30).

10. Arius, *Letter to Alexander of Alexandria*, 4 (Rusch, 32).

11. Ibid., 2–3 (Rusch, 31).

12. Ibid., 2 (Rusch, 31).

13. Arius, *Letter to Eusebius of Nicomedia*, 5 (Rusch, 30).

14. Arius, *Thalia*; quoted in Athanasius, *Orations against the Arians*, I, 6 (Rusch, 67).

15. Arius, *Thalia*; quoted in Athanasius, *On the Councils*, 15. Translation from Rowan Williams, *Arius: Heresy and Tradition* (London: Darton, Longman and Todd, 1987), 102.

16. Arius, *Thalia*; quoted in Athanasius, *Orations against the Arians*, I, 6 (Rusch, 68).

17. Admittedly, at the end of the film—I won't spoil it—Disney seemingly forgot they were making an extended parable about subordinationist theology...but you get the idea.

18. Arius, *Letter to Alexander of Alexandria*, 2 (Rusch, 31).

19. Arius, *Letter to Eusebius of Nicomedia*, 3 (Rusch, 29).

20. Origen, *Commentary on John*, II, 2 and 6.

21. Quoted in Eusebius of Caesarea, *The Life of Constantine*, 66. The translation used here may be found in Philip Schaff and Henry Wace, eds., *Nicene and Post-Nicene Fathers*, series 2, vol. 1: *Eusebius: Church History, Life of Constantine the Great, and Oration in Praise of Constantine* (Peabody, MA: Hendrickson, [1890] 1994), 481–580.

22. Ibid., 71.

23. Eusebius of Caesarea has left us his own account of what transpired at Nicaea. While an interesting and revealing document in many ways, it may not unfairly be described, like Krusty the Klown's autobiography, as "self-serving with many glaring omissions." See his *Letter to the Church of Caesarea* (Rusch, 57–69).

24. Arius, *Letter to Eusebius of Nicomedia*, 2 (Rusch, 29).

25. Arius, *Thalia*; quoted in Athanasius, *Orations against the Arians*, I, 6 (Rusch, 67).

26. Arius, *Letter to Alexander of Alexandria*, 2 (Rusch, 31).

27. Arius, *Thalia*; quoted in Athanasius, *On the Councils*, 15. Translation from Williams, *Arius*, 102.

28. For instance, he ascribes the idea that the Son is like "a light from a light as a lamp divided in two" to the heretic Hieracas of Leontopolis, an Egyptian Gnostic of the third century. See Arius, *Letter to Alexander of Alexandria*, 2 (Rusch, 31).

29. Rusch, 49.

30. Athanasius, *Orations against the Arians*, I, 6 (Rusch, 69).

31. Alexander, *Letter to Alexander of Thessalonica*, 4 (Rusch, 33).

32. Ibid., 17 (Rusch, 36).

33. Gregory of Nazianzus, *Third Theological Oration* (or *Oration* 29), 18 (Rusch, 144).

34. Ibid.

35. Athanasius, *Life of St Anthony*, 69. The translation used here may be found in Philip Schaff and Henry Wace, eds., *Nicene and Post-Nicene Fathers*, series 2, vol. 4: *Athanasius: Select Works and Letters* (Peabody, MA: Hendrickson, [1890] 1994), 195–221. Strictly speaking, Athanasius quotes these words from the desert father Anthony of Egypt (who, for an unlettered hermit, betrays an impressive knowledge of the minutiae of the Arian controversy). The reader is left in no doubt, however, that Athanasius himself agrees with them.

36. Athanasius, *Orations against the Arians*, I, 9 (Rusch, 70).
37. John McDade, "Preaching the Trinity," *Pastoral Review* 10, no. 3 (May/June 2014): 28.
38. Ibid., I, 43 (Rusch, 106).
39. Ibid., I, 42 (Rusch, 105).
40. Gregory of Nazianzus, *Third Theological Oration* (or *Oration* 29), 19 (Rusch, 144).
41. Arianism continued to flourish outside of the Roman Empire, for example among Germanic tribes such as the Goths and Vandals. Hence from the fifth century onward, Arians posed a greater military threat to the harmony and unity of the Church and empire than they did a theological one.
42. Basil the Great, *On the Holy Spirit*, XXX, 7. The translation used here may be found in Philip Schaff and Henry Wace, eds., *Nicene and Post-Nicene Fathers*, series 2, vol. 8: *Basil: Letters and Select Works* (Peabody, MA: Hendrickson, [1890] 1994), 1–50.
43. Gregory of Nazianzus, *Fifth Theological Oration* (or *Oration* 31), 10. Translation from Gregory of Nazianzus, *On God and Christ: The Five Theological Orations and Two Letters to Cledonius*, trans. Frederick Williams and Lionel Wickham (New York: St. Vladimir's Seminary Press, 2002), 123.

6

WHY NOT
THREE GODS?

This chapter does not narrate any definable "crisis." While statements 2 and 3 of our trilemma were tested in the "furnace of blazing fire" (Dan 3:6) of ecclesial strife, statement 1 ("There is only one God") was treated in the *relative* "cool of the day" (Gen 3:8, NIV) of theological speculation. This in itself testifies to the Church's developed confidence in its apprehension of who God is, and in its ability to express this in a not wholly imperfect manner, by the late fourth century. Not coincidentally, this was also an age of true theological greats. We have met Athanasius, Basil, and Gregory of Nazianzus already. Gregory of Nyssa will star in this chapter; Augustine, and to a lesser extent Hilary and Jerome, in the next.[1]

Though there was never a "controversy" analogous to those produced by modalism and Arianism, *accusations* of tritheism (i.e., belief in the existence of three gods) were common in the whole period we have been exploring. As seen in chapter 4, Tertullian complained in the early third century that "they put it about that by us two or even three gods are preached, while they, they claim, are worshippers of one God."[2] The best part of two centuries later, Gregory of Nazianzus wearily admits that the charge is still current: "If, it is asserted, we use the word 'God' three times, must there not be three Gods?"[3] By affirming *both* the distinction between Father, Son, and Holy Spirit (against the modalists), *and* the full divinity of each of them (against the Arians), it is claimed that mainstream Christianity is a de facto denial of the oneness of God: if the three are truly three, and each is truly God, then surely there must be three Gods. In the terms of our trilemma, then, the allegation looks like this:

1. There is only one God.
2. The Father, the Son, and the Holy Spirit is each God.
3. The Father, the Son, and the Holy Spirit are not the same.

In fact, unlike the other heresies we have looked at, tritheism seems never to have been a live option in our whole period. Though many were accused of having lapsed, unwittingly or not, into affirming three gods, we have no reliable evidence that anyone ever claimed the position as their own. True, later Christian history throws up the occasional individual who seems to fit the bill. Yet even then, one struggles to identify unambiguously tritheistic movements or schisms.

Nevertheless, orthodox theologians were properly enough concerned with the *theoretical* danger of tritheism. In stating quite confidently that Father, Son, and Holy Spirit is each true God, they certainly did not want to deny—or tempt others to deny—what "even the demons" know full well, "that God is one" (Jas 2:19). They needed a *coherent* way of affirming, as the Athanasian Creed puts it, that "the Father is God, the Son is God, the Holy Spirit is God. And yet there is, not three gods, but one God."[4] We will see how they found it, using concepts ultimately pioneered by Tertullian (albeit in a different language), and led by Basil's brother, St. Gregory of Nyssa, in due course. However, first, it is worth detouring with a brief "flashback" to think more deeply about a number of issues.

▲ ▲ ▲

Traditional Roman religion, like that of the Greeks, was characterized by a multiplicity of gods. Big gods and little gods, male gods and female gods, public gods and private gods...ranging in role from celestial warrior-kings (e.g., *Sol Invictus* or "the Unconquered Sun") to mild-mannered civil engineers ("the god who invented roads and pathways," as charmingly invoked in a second-century inscription from—where else?—England). For an expansionist empire, absorbing disparate peoples and cultures into a hopefully harmonious *Pax Romana*, such a flexible divine ecology was handy. The local divinities of conquered lands could be easily partnered with existing Roman ones (thus the Celtic water goddess, Sulis, and the Turkish war god, Dolichenus, became naturalized Roman citizens as Sulis

Minerva and Jupiter Dolichenus). Every so often, an exotic novelty might pique the Romans' jaded devotional palate—for example, Egypt's Isis or Asia Minor's Mithras—and this, too, would be added to the official state *pantheon* or "all the gods."

As previously mentioned, the Jews' refusal to allow either "the Lᴏʀᴅ God, the Holy One of Israel" (Isa 30:15) to be domesticated into the Roman cultus, or the Roman gods to contaminate the temple liturgy, truly set them apart within the empire's occupied peoples: "There shall be no strange god among you; you shall not bow down to a foreign god" (Ps 81:9). Tragically and heroically, it was a refusal for which they paid a heavy price in the year 70.

This double context is important to grasp when thinking about early Christian apologetics. Christ's advent was seen as bringing *both* "revelation to the Gentiles" *and* "glory to your people Israel" (Luke 2:31–32). However, Rome and Jerusalem each presented very different theological soils in which to sow the Word. Since they shared the Jewish disdain for the classical gods—"what pagans sacrifice, they sacrifice to demons" (1 Cor 10:20)—the Romans saw Christians not as monotheists or even tritheists, but rather as a particularly pernicious brand of *atheists*.[5] Jews, meanwhile, regarded the Nazarenes' worship of Christ and the Spirit alongside the Father as proof of pagan polytheism—an impression that was no doubt reinforced by their swift abandoning of Jewish customs and rapid growth courtesy of Gentile conversions.

This produced a discernible tension in the writings of the greatest of second-century apologists, St. Justin Martyr. As a Gentile convert, Justin's own meandering journey to the faith—which led him ultimately to the martyr's crown—was jointly influenced by Greek philosophy and Hebrew prophecy.[6] Accordingly, in Justin's surviving works we see him address both Gentiles and Jews. Speaking to the former, he criticizes the "soulless and dead"[7] idols of Roman polytheism—"Those who believe these things we pity, and those who invented them we know to be devils"[8]—while affirming "the most true God"[9] to whom "alone we render worship."[10] Meanwhile, when seeking to convince Jews of the divinity of Christ, he says things like this: "I shall attempt to persuade you, since you have understood the Scriptures...that there is, and that there is said to be, *another God* and Lord subject to the Maker of all things."[11]

Justin's problem is that he is simultaneously trying to convince the Romans that there is only one God, while demonstrating to the Jews that both the Father and the Son are really God. It is no wonder, then, that he occasionally veers into some (with the joyous benefit of hindsight) dubious-sounding phraseology. That Justin doesn't really *mean* "another" in the sense of there being *two* is clear from his earlier assurances to his Jewish dialogue partner that

> there will be no other God, O Trypho, nor was there from eternity any other existing, but He who made and disposed all this universe. Nor do we think that there is one God for us, another for you, but that He alone is God who led your fathers out from Egypt with a strong hand and a high arm. Nor have we trusted in any other (for there is no other), but in Him in whom you also have trusted, the God of Abraham, and of Isaac, and of Jacob.[12]

Likewise, his explanation to his Roman audience that Christians confess only the "most true God, the Father of righteousness"[13] mustn't be understood as an avowal of unitarianism, for he is equally up-front about the fact that they "worship and adore" also "the Son of the true God himself...and the prophetic Spirit."[14] Reading both within and between the lines, one can see what Justin is *trying* to state. He is, as we have been putting it, trying *to say all three things at once.* Yet in the mid-second century—at least fifty years before Tertullian and Hippolytus enter the trinitarian fray, let alone Athanasius and the Cappadocian fathers—he doesn't yet have an adequate terminology to make this statement.

▲ ▲ ▲

Fast-forward nearly a quarter of a millennium to 390 or thereabouts, nine years or so after the Council of Constantinople. Gregory, bishop of Nyssa in central Turkey, brother of Basil (and *three* other saints), and close comrade of Gregory of Nazianzus, receives a question from his younger friend Ablabius.[15] Ablabius's problem is this: Peter, James, and John all share the same human nature. In other words, unlike Geppetto and Pinocchio, they are indeed *homoousios* with each other and are quite naturally called

82

three men. However, if that is so, then why aren't the Father, the Son, and the Holy Spirit, since all share the one divine nature, likewise called *three gods*? Note that Ablabius, "noble soldier of Christ,"[16] is not suggesting that they should be so called. Rather, he is worried that the terminology the Church had come to use for speaking about the Trinity might not be adequate after all. Gregory, he has every reason to hope, is the man to put his fears to rest.

Gregory, for his part, immediately perceives the significance of the question:

> This is not a minor subject which you have put forward for us, nor is it of such a kind to cause slight damage.... The force of the enquiry necessarily brings one into one of two altogether incompatible positions...to say that there are three gods, which is wicked [or] not to bear witness to the deity of the Son and the Spirit, which is ungodly and absurd.[17]

Christian doctrine seems to be caught between the frying pan of tritheism and the fire of Arianism. And like Justin before him, Gregory must defend oneness and threeness simultaneously against both sides of this "strange dilemma."[18] Before doing so, he offers an instructive sidelight onto his theological method: "If our reasoning would be proven unequal to the task, we will guard the tradition we received from the fathers as always firm and immovable....On the basis of what is known we will keep the unchangeable faith."[19] Here, Gregory expresses his conviction that the oneness of God, the divinity of the three persons, and their distinctness one from another—that is to say, the constituent parts of our trinitarian trilemma—are revealed truths, lovingly preserved by sacred tradition. As a bishop and theologian, it is Gregory's task to explore and elucidate the faith. If he cannot do so adequately, then that is more a comment on his own flawed powers than on his chosen subject matter. And indeed, among the Church fathers he is one of those most alive to the *limits* of human reason and speech in trespassing on the divine (cf. chapter 1). As he writes to Ablabius, "We say that every name, whether it has been invented from human usage or handed down from Scripture, is an interpretation of the things thought about divine nature and does not encompass the significance of the nature itself."[20] With those caveats in place, Gregory sets about his task.

▲ ▲ ▲

Ablabius's question—and Gregory's answer to it—revolve around some technical vocabulary. We saw in chapter 3 how Tertullian began speaking of the Father, Son, and Holy Spirit as three "persons" (*personae*) in one "nature" (*substantia*). Tertullian was writing in Latin, while most of the following years' controversies were conducted in Greek. Over time, an analogous terminology developed in Greek too, using the concepts of *hypostasis* and *ousia*. *Ousia*, as we saw in the last chapter, means "nature" or "substance," as in Nicaea's signature term *homoousios* ("of the same nature" or, in Latinized English, "consubstantial"). Very confusingly, *hypostasis* could mean more or less the same thing: thus when Origen or Arius spoke of "three *hypostases*" they are referring to three separate natures.[21] And it was in *this* sense that Nicaea condemned the opinion that "that the Son of God is of another *hypostasis* or *ousia*."

By the time Ablabius and Gregory were corresponding, however, *hypostasis* had come to be used rather differently. Here, *hypostasis* means a concrete instance (or perhaps better, "instantiation") of an *ousia*. For example, there are currently three chairs in my office, each dissimilar from the others: one has wheels, while the others do not; one is low, and green, and covered in faux leather, while the others are not; and so on. Despite these differences, they all share certain essential properties of a chair (e.g., they have a seat and a back, and are primarily intended and used for sitting on). If we were of a certain kind of philosophical mindset, we might say that they all participate in the nature or essence of "chairness." Or rather, that they are three *hypostases* ("instantiations") of the one Chair-y *ousia*. Though distinct, they all share the same fundamental nature—that is to say, they are *homoousios* or consubstantial with each other. Likewise, when we speak of Peter, James, and John as three *hypostases* of the one human *ousia*, we mean that they are three instantiations of "humanness"— three specific instances of the one Humanity. Note that Peter, James, and John do not divide or "share out" their common human nature. Each is fully and completely human; they are not "one-third human" because there are three of them (or indeed a "several-billionth human" because there have been several billion humans throughout history). The human *ousia* subsists fully in each *hypostasis*.

Applying this to the Trinity results in three *hypostases*, each of whom participate in the same, singular divine *ousia*: the Father, the Son, and the Holy Spirit are all instantiations of the one "Godhead" (a word that comes from the Middle English word, *godhede*, meaning Godhood or "God-ness"). "In Godhead one, in persons three," as the hymn puts it. Or as Gregory of Nyssa writes in an earlier work, "While we confess three persons [*hypostases*] we say that there is one goodness, and one power, and one Godhead."[22] Again, it is important to note that each is not a "third" of God; the Godhead subsists fully in each *hypostasis*. Thus as the *Catholic Catechism* quotes from our other Gregory, he of Nazianzus: "Each person considered in himself is entirely God."[23]

If you're finding this distinction between *hypostasis* and *ousia* difficult to grasp, then take comfort from the fact that you are in fine company. Augustine, himself no theological slouch, complains that "the Greeks...make a distinction that is rather obscure to me between *ousia* and *hypostasis*."[24] Accordingly, Augustine prefers his Latin terms *substantia* (or sometimes *natura* or *essentia*) and *persona*, as had Tertullian some two centuries earlier.[25] Each term has its own shades of meanings, and own histories in the writings of earlier theologians, orthodox or otherwise. In the next chapter, we will have more to say on the limits of all such seemingly very precise terms, when attempting to describe the inner life of the "King of glory" (Ps 24:7). For now, though, let us be content that what Greek-speaking Gregory means by "three *hypostases* in one *ousia*" is the same as what Latin-speaking Augustine means by "three *personae* in one *substantia*," and that both are equivalent to "three persons in one nature," as it is usually expressed in English.

Sticking with the Greek, which is after all what Gregory and Ablabius were using, this all provides a rather neat-looking solution to our trinitarian trilemma:

1. There is only one God (i.e., there is a single divine *ousia*).
2. The Father, the Son, and the Holy Spirit is each God (i.e., each fully shares the same divine *ousia*).

3. The Father, the Son, and the Holy Spirit are not the same (i.e., they constitute three distinct *hypostases* of the same divine *ousia*).

In essence, this is what the Christian Church decided was the orthodox solution to the trilemma presented to it by Scripture (and thus ultimately, as argued in chapters 2 and 3, by God's own self-revelation). This is how to "say all three things at once." *This is how not to be a heretic.*

At least, it would be...but only once the Church was convinced that it didn't imply tritheism.

▲ ▲ ▲

The precise problem Ablabius posed to Gregory, it is worth recalling, was this:

Peter, James, and John, being in one humanity, are called three men....If therefore usage here permits this...how, in reference to the mystical beliefs in the confession that there are three *hypostases*, and the claim that there is no difference between them in nature, do we struggle with the confession by declaring there is one deity of Father, Son, and Spirit but by forbidding the statement that there are three gods?[26]

Gregory's first move, to put it mildly, is something of a bold opening gambit: he denies the premise of the question. Strictly speaking, he argues, it is "an abuse of usage when those who are not determined by nature...are named in the plural."[27] That is to say, Peter, James, and John *aren't* really "three men" at all. *Man* refers to the single human nature that is fully possessed by each of them. Accordingly, the plural term *men* implies that "there are many human natures."[28] Yet this cannot be:

But the nature (*ousia*) is one; it is united to itself, undivided, continuous, perfect, and not divided by those who individually share it. And just as...an army, or an assembly is always mentioned as singular but each is discovered

86

in the plural, so in accord with the most precise reasoning also "man" properly should be said as one (singular), even if those shown to be in the same nature would be plural.[29]

It is not the nature that is plural, but the instantiations of that nature. Hence, one should speak not of three men, but rather of three human *hypostases*. (In Latin, of course, this works even better: we can speak of three human *personae*, or "persons").

Gregory is well aware of how strange some of this must sound. And he isn't seriously suggesting that we stop talking about "men"—or anything else to which the same argument applies—in this way. (For example, I would have to start saying that there are "three chair-y *hypostases*" or "three instantiations of the one Chairness" in my office, instead of "three chairs.") He happily admits such "improvement of usage" would be both impractical and impossible, especially when "there is no loss here in the wrong employment of words."[30] While talk of three men or three chairs might be somewhat loose, philosophically speaking, there's no real harm in it...*except*, that is, when we allow the same imprecision to be carried over into theological matters: "In reference to the divine doctrine, the indifferent employment of words is no longer, similarly, without danger, for here 'minor' points are not minor."[31] As Gregory notes, even Scripture is happy to submit to

> the custom of prevailing language [when speaking of such things where] no damage concerning the intention of words is involved....But where there is a danger that something of the truth could be damaged, no longer does one find in the written words an unquestioning and indifferent state of affairs.[32]

He cites here the self-same example we have remarked upon several times: that the Scriptures refer directly to both Father and Son as "God" (e.g., John 1), but is careful never to speak of them as "two Gods." He further points out that this applies not only to the term *God* itself, but to a range of other divine attributes also: "Just as the nature is said to be one, all the other aspects are named individually in the singular, God, good, holy, saviour, righteous judge, and whatever other names befitting God come to mind."[33]

▲ ▲ ▲

So far, so good, although perhaps one can't help feeling that Gregory has moved the goalposts a little. Asked to explain why Father, Son, and Holy Spirit are not three gods, he has instead shown that Peter, James, and John are not in fact three men. Even though we might concede the point, Gregory has yet to offer a *better* analogy for talking about the Trinity.[34] Is there anything in "the custom of the prevailing language" that would help and not hinder us in understanding "divine doctrine"?

There certainly is. For example, Gregory suggests the case of gold: "When we speak of gold, even if it is changed into many [different things], still it is, and is mentioned as, one."[35]

Gregory's own example is of coins, but I think the point is even clearer if we imagine three distinct objects. Imagine, let us say, a key, a ring, and a crucifix, all made of pure, unalloyed gold. Though obviously distinct—the key is not the ring, the ring is not the crucifix, the crucifix is not the key—they all share the same basic nature, at least so far as their "goldenness" is concerned. Furthermore, the essential properties of goldenness subsist fully in all three of them: their atoms' nuclei contain precisely seventy-nine protons, each will dissolve in aqua regia, and so on. They are thus, in our terminology, three instantiations (*hypostases/personae*) of the one golden nature (*ousia/substantia*).[36]

So the ring is gold, the key is gold, and the crucifix is gold: they are *homoousios* in their goldenness. *But here's the point:* "It is properly said not that there are 'many golds' but that there are 'many golden ones'"[37] In both Greek and English, it just *sounds* odd to say "three golds": ordinary usage dictates that we speak of "three golden objects" or "three things made out of gold." And on this point, Gregory notes that the "prevailing custom" is accurate, as it isn't when referring to men: "Therefore just as the golden [objects] are many but gold is one, thus those who are individually in the nature of man are revealed as many, for example, Peter, James, and John. But the 'man' in them is

88

one."[38] And much more to the point, something similar is true when we speak of the Trinity.

In fact, Gregory's gold analogy works even better in English than it does in Greek. Consider the following:

1. There is only one Gold (i.e., there is a single golden *ousia*).
2. The key, the ring, and the crucifix is each Gold (i.e., each fully shares the same golden *ousia*).
3. The key, the ring, and the crucifix are not the same (i.e., they constitute three distinct *hypostases* of the same golden *ousia*).

This provides us with a perfectly normal, everyday example of talk about a single essence that is fully realized in three ways. Naturally, it would sound quite as weird to insist that the key, the ring, and the crucifix must therefore be identical, as it would to say, "Well, if there are three golden objects, there must be, therefore, three *golds*." Gregory is not, of course, saying that the divine persons are actually like golden trinkets, or anything of the sort. However, he *is* saying that the grammar of the Trinity is not necessarily so far opposed to ordinary language as we might think. And while some analogies might mislead us (e.g., that of "three men"), others can help us see that the Church's slowly, and indeed, at times, rather painfully, developed way of "saying all three things at once" is not at all non-sensical.

▲ ▲ ▲

Gregory's argument appears to have worked, because any lingering misgivings over the *hypostasis/ousia*—along with the more-or-less Latin equivalent, *persona/substantia*—terminology were sufficiently allayed for it to become solidly established by the early fifth century. This was how the universal Church discerned that it could best remain faithful to the self-revelation of God, first in human history, and second in the Scriptures, which both testify to and reflect upon that history: "Everyone then who hears these words of mine and acts on them will be like a wise man who built his house on rock. The rain fell, the floods came, and the winds blew and beat on that house, but it did not fall, because it had been founded on rock"

(Matt 7:24–25). Along the way, modalism, Arianism, and a healthy paranoia about lapsing into tritheism were not simply countered, *but had been learned from.*

Admittedly, this is not quite the end of our journey: trinitarian theologizing, and indeed its controversy, naturally did not end with the closing of the fourth century. Nevertheless, we have reached a significant landmark, and it is well worth our pausing a moment.

What we have been calling the *trinitarian trilemma* is simply an attempt to underline the fact that the *basic content* of the doctrine of the Trinity—if not necessarily its expression, or its many implications—is really and truly very simple indeed. To recap:

1. There is only one God (i.e., there is a single divine *ousia*).
2. The Father, the Son, and the Holy Spirit is each God (i.e., each fully shares the same divine *ousia*).
3. The Father, the Son, and the Holy Spirit are not the same (i.e., they constitute three distinct *hypostases* of the same divine *ousia*)

Hopefully, this has proven a helpful heuristic in grasping what is really essential here (as it has for me, over the years). If not, the Christian tradition offers us plenty of others, and ones whose authors are infinitely more worthy of attention than is the trilemma's.

Take, for example, Gregory of Nazianzus's terse summary spoken at the Council of Constantinople in 381:

We believe...in the Father, the Son and the Holy Spirit, of one substance and glory...acknowledging the Unity in the *ousia* and in the undivided worship, and the Trinity in the *hypostases* or persons (which term some prefer).[39]

Or consider, at greater length and much more didactically, these excerpts from the (Latin) Athanasian Creed:[40]

We worship one God in Trinity, and Trinity in Unity; neither confounding persons [*personae*], nor separating essence [*substantia*]. For there is one person of the Father, another of the Son, and another of the Holy Spirit. But the Father, and the Son, and the Holy Spirit is one Godhead [*divinitas*], the glory equal, the majesty coeternal....The Father is God, the Son is God, the Holy Spirit is God. And yet there is, not three gods, but one God.

This, the Creed tells us, "is the Catholic Faith." Or in other words: affirming the above concerning the Trinity is precisely *how not to be a heretic*.

Notes

1. Also adding Cyril of Jerusalem, Ambrose of Milan, John Chrysostom, and—moving into the first half of the fifth century—John Cassian, Leo the Great, and Cyril of Alexandria, one can see why people often speak here of a "golden age."

2. Tertullian, *Against Praxeas*, 1. See also Origen, *Commentary on John*, II, 2.

3. Gregory of Nazianzus, *Fifth Theological Oration* (or *Oration* 31), 13. Translation from Gregory of Nazianzus, *On God and Christ: The Five Theological Orations and Two Letters to Cledonius*, trans. Frederick Williams and Lionel Wickham (New York: St. Vladimir's Seminary Press, 2002), 127.

4. This Latin creed, probably dating from the late fifth or sixth century, was mistakenly attributed to Athanasius in the medieval period (presumably due to both its, and his, clear and uncompromisingly orthodox presentation of the doctrine of the Trinity). In fact, its phrasing has more directly in common with the writings of Latin Fathers such as Augustine and—following his lead—St. Vincent of Lérins and St. Caesarius of Arles. It is regarded as authoritative by the Catholic Church, as also by many mainstream Protestant denominations.

5. I have written at length on this topic in a previous book. Please see chapter 1 of *Faith and Unbelief* (Paulist Press, 2014).

6. See Justin Martyr, *Dialogue with Trypho*, 2–8. All translations from Justin's writings here are taken from Alexander Roberts and James Donaldson, eds., *The Ante-Nicene Fathers*, vol. 1: *The*

Apostolic Fathers, Justin Martyr, Irenaeus (Edinburgh: T. & T. Clark, [1885] 1996).

7. Justin Martyr, *First Apology*, 9.

8. Ibid., 25.

9. Ibid., 6.

10. Ibid., 17.

11. Justin Martyr, *Dialogue with Trypho*, 56; emphasis added.

12. Ibid., 11.

13. Ibid., 6.

14. Ibid., 6, 13.

15. All references to Gregory's reply to Ablabius, often titled either *Ad Ablabium* or simply *On Not Three Gods*, will be given from the translation included in William G. Rusch, ed. and trans., *The Trinitarian Controversy* (Philadelphia: Fortress Press, 1980). Page references to this translation will be given in parentheses. Unlike most of the other patristic sources quoted in this book, the standard English translations do not subdivide the text by chapter/paragraph numbers.

16. Gregory of Nyssa, *On Not Three Gods* (Rusch, 149).

17. Ibid.

18. Ibid., (Rusch, 150).

19. Ibid.

20. Ibid., (Rusch, 152).

21. Arius, *Letter to Alexander*, 4 (Rusch, 31); see also Origen, *Commentary on John*, II, 6.

22. Gregory of Nyssa, *On the Holy Trinity (Letter to Eustathius)*. The translation used here may be found in Philip Schaff and Henry Wace, eds., *Nicene and Post-Nicene Fathers*, series 2, vol. 5: *Gregory of Nyssa: Dogmatic Treatises, etc.* (Peabody, MA: Hendrickson, [1890] 1994), 326–30.

23. *Catechism of the Catholic Church* 256; quoting Gregory of Nazianzus, *Oration* 40, 41.

24. Augustine, *On the Trinity*, V, 10. Translation from *The Trinity*, trans. Edmund Hill (Brooklyn, NY: New City Press, 1991), 196.

25. See Lewis Ayres, *Augustine and the Trinity* (Cambridge: Cambridge University Press, 2010), 79–82.

26. Gregory of Nyssa, *On Not Three Gods* (Rusch, 149–50).

27. Ibid., (Rusch, 150).

28. Ibid.
29. Ibid., (Rusch, 151).
30. Ibid.
31. Ibid.
32. Ibid., (Rusch, 158–59).
33. Ibid., (Rusch, 159).
34. At least, he hasn't "yet" in the way we are (re)structuring his overall argument here. In the original text itself—and please do read it yourself—he gives the example I'm just about to describe *before* he makes the point about the Scriptures that I just have quoted.
35. Gregory of Nyssa, *On Not Three Gods* (Rusch, 158).
36. Each is also, individually, an instantiation of "keyness," "ringness," and "crucificity"—but that is by the bye.
37. Gregory of Nyssa, *On Not Three Gods* (Rusch, 158).
38. Ibid.
39. Gregory of Nazianzus, *Oration* 42, 16. The translation used here may be found in Philip Schaff and Henry Wace, eds., *Nicene and Post-Nicene Fathers* series 2, vol. 7: *Cyril of Jerusalem, Gregory Nazianzen* (Peabody, MA: Hendrickson, [1890] 1994), 385–95.
40. See endnote 4, above.

7

THREE
WHAT?

Three *hypostases* in one *ousia*. Three *personae* in one *substantia*. Three persons in one nature. *Instantiation, homoousios, consubstantial, trinity*....We have come a very long way from the childish scribblings of chapter 1, humbly confessing with Anselm and Thomas our flawed and fallen attempts "to fathom the wonders of the Lord" (Sir 18:6). Six chapters on, we have a set of precise, technical jargon, such as might appear on an engineer's blueprint. Now we can minutely describe the inner life of "the High God" (Deut 33:12), in three languages no less, and—like a mechanic discoursing on the inner workings of a car—sound like we really know our stuff.

Before we get too carried away in our "proud glory" (Lev 26:19), we might profit from the words of a fifteenth-century monk, Thomas à Kempis: "Of what use is it to discourse learnedly on the Trinity, if you lack humility and therefore displease the Trinity?"[1] Accordingly, our purpose here is to balance sincere appreciation of the grand theological achievement of the first four Christian centuries with a sober admission of the undeniable constraints we face in broaching the One "we can never think about...as he deserves," and whom "no words of ours are capable of expressing."[2] Those latter phrases are taken from St. Augustine of Hippo's influential *On the Trinity* (or *De Trinitate*, to give its often-used original title). Writing in the early fifth century— within decades of the Council of Constantinople (381) and the deaths of Basil (379), Gregory of Nazianzus (c. 390), and Gregory of Nyssa (c. 395)—Augustine did not simply synthesize the previous centuries' insights. Rather, applying his own genius, he built upon them. As we turn now to probe some lingering issues, mostly to do with language and its limits, Augustine will serve as a trusty companion and guide.

We will focus on three topics in particular: the dangers lurking in such jargon as *person* and *hypostasis*; how the Father, Son, and Spirit are and are not distinct (which will prompt us to introduce one final piece of jargon: *filioque*); and the acute problems thrown up by gender.

▲ ▲ ▲

Augustine's confusion over the Greek-speakers' use of *hypostasis* was noted in the previous chapter. As we have seen, he followed Tertullian and many other Latin speakers in preferring *persona* ("person") to denote each member of the Trinity. It is largely through his influence that it became the go-to terminology among Western Christians ever after. However, Augustine was under no illusions as to its explanatory power or precision—nor should we be:

> In very truth, because the Father is not the Son and the Son is not the Father, and the Holy Spirit...is neither the Father nor the Son, they are certainly three....Yet when you ask "Three what?" human speech labors under a great dearth of words. So we say three persons, not in order to say precisely, but in order not to be reduced to silence.[3]

The word *person* is preferred, *not* because we know it to be a perfect and accurate description, but because we *hope* that it is less imperfect and inaccurate than the other options. As he puts it later, we speak of persons "simply in order to be able to say something when asked 'Three what?'"[4] If nothing else, Augustine remarks wryly, it is better than saying "three somethings."[5]

Augustine is in harmony here with several of his *hypostasis*-preferring "Greek colleagues."[6] Gregory of Nyssa's views on the relative significance of theological talk, *even Scripture's*, when compared to what it is actually striving to talk about, were briefly quoted in the last chapter. Gregory of Nazianzus, for his part, gave short shrift to those who get overly hung up on differences in phraseology "as if our faith depended on words and not on realities."[7] Amen to that: for to be sure, neither *hypostasis* nor *person* is especially satisfactory. The former probably sounded as dry and abstract in ancient Greek as do *instantiation* or *subsistence* in modern English. And while the latter at least implies something, well, more *personal*—which is certainly faithful to the Trinity's own self-revelation in Scripture— the noun itself is potentially even more misleading when applied to the Godhead.

The problem is this: we tend to think of *person* as signifying an independent individual, separate from all other, equally independent individuals. Even *if* Gregory is right that Peter, James, and John are not strictly "three men," we must at least view them as being three self-contained, autonomous subjects: "Three centers of conscious-ness and activity,"[8] as Karl Rahner once put it. It is often said that this is a peculiarly modern, post-Enlightenment conception of *per-son*; I am not so sure.[9] Nonetheless, while the Father, the Son, and the Holy Spirit must be thought of as genuinely distinct, the Christian tradition has never wanted to imagine them as being remotely *that* distinct. Think especially here of some of those pas-sages in John:

The Father and I are one. (10:30)

I am in the Father and the Father is in me. (14:11)

When the Spirit of truth comes...he will glorify me, because he will take what is mine and declare it to you. All that the Father has is mine. For this reason I said that he will take what is mine and declare it to you. (16:13–15)

However we are to get our heads around these "figures of speech" (John 16:25), the divine persons are hardly depicted as a loose coali-tion of individuals. Since the three "really are three,"[10] there must be some sense in which they resemble a kind of community or society.[11] Nevertheless, Christian theology mustn't lose sight of the genuine, substantial unity of the three either. The One really *is* one, too.

But how do we safeguard the oneness and threeness alike? How to distinguish without dividing, differentiate but not separate?

From Tertullian and Hippolytus onward, the fathers offer multiple analogies for getting *some* sense of how this should be imagined. Suggestions range from the relatively simple (e.g., a conjoined spring, river, and canal; or the sun, its beams, and the illumination they give[12]), to the decidedly complex (e.g., the constituent parts of the mind making up a unified consciousness[13]). However, every one of their proponents would, it must be stressed, wholeheartedly echo St. Hilary of Poitiers' warning: "Let no one suppose such analogies are perfect and complete....We must therefore regard any comparison as helpful to man rather than as descriptive of God, since it suggests, rather than exhausts, the sense we seek."[14]

Analogies aside, there is a reasonable consensus among the fathers that one way of affirming the tri-*unity* is by resisting the urge to carve up the divine activity between the three persons. Father, Son, and Holy Spirit are not three lone operators who, like the Three Amigos, *occasionally* team up to create the universe, or afterward redeem it. Rather, in the words of Gregory of Nyssa, "Every activity which pervades from God to creation...starts off from the Father, proceeds through the Son, and is completed by the Holy Spirit....The action of each in any regard is not divided and peculiar."[15] Augustine agrees, although the real trick—and one he admits taxes him "to the point of weariness"—is to find a way of affirming that "the Trinity works inseparably in everything God works," and yet avoiding modalism while explaining

> how that utterance which was only the Father's was caused by the three; and how that flesh in which only the Son was born of the virgin was created by the same three; and how that form of the dove in which only the Holy Spirit appeared was fashioned by the Trinity itself. Otherwise the Trinity does not work inseparably.[16]

▲ ▲ ▲

This raises a further, yet knottier problem. Even if activity *were* the way to distinguish the persons, then what differentiated them "before all ages"—that is, before there was a creation for them to act within? Or to put it another way, do the Father, Son, and Holy Spirit differ *among themselves*—or only in the ways they relate to us?

Now, one way of answering this question is to imagine some kind of hierarchy within the Godhead. Most obviously, this would place the Father atop the divine podium, with the Son and Spirit on the silver and bronze steps. Some early theologians toyed with this kind of approach. However, no doubt influenced by the fight against Arius's brand of subordinationism, this soon fell out of favor. Gregory of Nazianzus puts the prevailing view best:

> The Son does not fall short in some particular of being Father. Sonship is no defect, yet that does not mean he *is* Father. By the same token, the Father would fall short of being Son—the Father is *not* Son. No, the language here gives no grounds for any deficiency, for any subordination in being.[17]

As Gregory hints here, a more satisfactory response is perhaps to be found in the *relationships* within the Godhead: "We say there is no deficiency—God lacks nothing. It is in their difference in, so to speak, 'manifestation' or mutual relationship, which has caused the difference in names."[18]

Think again of the Prologue to John's Gospel. The evangelist presents us with two distinct persons, each of whom is described as God (1:1). These are named as *Father* and *Son*, with the latter said to be "begotten" of the former (1:14, 18). Such terms are, of course, metaphors patterned on biological generation and relationships. We understand what it means for a human *father* to *beget* a *son*, and we know the kind of mutual love, respect, concern, and closeness this relationship normally signifies. Hence there must be some sense in which a divine "father" eternally "begetting" a coequal "son" is somewhat, to *some* degree, like that. (As noted in chapter 1, we *must not* confuse a metaphor for a literal description.[19]) Remember also that, as Tertullian pointed out in chapter 4, Father and Son are themselves intrinsically *relational* terms: to call someone a *father* is to define him in terms of the child (or children) he is a father to; to call someone a *son* is to define him in terms of the parent (or parents) he is a son to. When transposed to the divine, such words function as what Jesus calls "figures of speech" (John 16:25). Nevertheless, these are the primary fingerholds that Scripture, following the Son's own lead, has given us to grasp how these two divine persons differ, and how they relate to each other. As such, it would seem that the Father and Son *are* genuinely to be distinguished with reference to their differing derivation (e.g., the Father begets the Son, but is not himself begotten, either by the Son or anyone else) and the relationships implied by it (e.g., the Son is not a Father; the Father is not a Son). In Augustine's pithy phrase, "Each is said with reference to the other."[20]

However, what of the Spirit? Here the relational plot really thickens. Since the Son is the only begotten (John 1:14, 18), the Spirit certainly cannot be a second Son—and is accordingly nowhere described as such in the Scriptures. In fact, here they abandon biological metaphors altogether and, it has to be said, leave very little in their place. The Spirit is, though, said to "go forth" or "proceed": "When the Advocate comes, whom I will send to you from the Father, the Spirit of truth who proceeds from the Father, he will testify on my behalf" (John 15:26, au. trans.). Thus, as the Athanasian Creed puts it, the Spirit is "neither made, nor created, nor begotten, but proceeding."

That is not, admittedly, a great deal to go on. *Procession* feels a fairly lackluster term to apply to the "spirit of Glory" (1 Pet 4:14). It is moreover not even exclusive to the Spirit: the Son says that *he* "proceeded from God" (John 8:42, au. trans.) too. The most we can state, therefore, is that the Spirit proceeds, but in a *different* way from how the Son proceeds (since the Son alone proceeds "begottenly," whatever that might mean).[21] If nothing else, this at least confirms the idea "the persons or *hypostases* are distinguished...by relations."[22] Again, all we can really say here is that the Spirit's relationship to the Father is *unlike* the Son's (i.e., it is not "filial"), and his relationship to the Son is *unlike* the Father's (i.e., it is not "paternal").

▲ ▲ ▲

As quoted in chapter 5, Constantinople included John's precise phrase "proceeds from the Father" in its updating of the Nicene Creed. Influenced by other scriptural evidence, not least the repeated claim that the Son *sends* the Spirit (John 15:26; 16:7), commentators had long affirmed that the Son must also have some role in the Spirit's procession. Diverse formulas had tried to capture this: for instance, witness Tertullian's "I believe the Spirit *to proceed* from no other source than from the Father *through the Son,*"[23] which proved popular in both West and East. Augustine, however, following Ambrose, came down strongly in favor of "from both the Father *and the Son.*"[24] In *On the Trinity*, it is clear he regards the scriptural evidence to be definitive on the theology undergirding "and the Son." This is especially true of the dual affirmation that he is both "the Spirit of [the] Father" (Matt 10:20) and "the Spirit of [the] Son" (Gal 4:6).[25] Nevertheless, Augustine seems not to be so concerned for the precise formula itself. His *Handbook on Faith, Hope, and Love*, likely written soon after the more densely doctrinal work, is happy to speak of "the Holy Spirit proceeding from...the Father, but one and the same Spirit of Father and Son."[26] Even for Augustine then, the exact phrasing is hardly a deal breaker.

Under Augustine's influence, the doctrine of "and the Son"— *filioque* in Latin—rapidly became standard in the West. Over the centuries, it began to creep into liturgical recitations of the Nicene Creed, perhaps by a kind of "pass the message"-style accident at first, but later with conviction. In the early ninth century, the Emperor Charlemagne petitioned Pope Leo III to add it officially into the Creed. Refusing to alter the creed of an ecumenical council (not that that had stopped the Fathers of Constantinople themselves, of course), Leo was nonetheless emphatic concerning the truth of the *filioque* doctrine itself.

"And the Son," and Augustine in general, fared less well in the East. This was not helped by the fact that, beginning in Augustine's own lifetime, the longstanding cultural and political ties between Latins and Greeks began slowly to crumble. While there had always been tensions and rivalries—not least between Rome, itself, and the gleaming "New Rome" of Constantinople, which became the imperial capital in 324—the gradual break-up of the western half of the empire, from the fifth century onward, led to ever-deepening estrangement. This meant that a certain brand of East-West ecclesial "sympathy in difference," apparent in Augustine or Gregory of Nazianzus, came to be in much shorter supply than in previous years. This did not happen immediately, of course. In the mid-seventh century, the Constantinopolitan monk-theologian, St. Maximus the Confessor, wrote knowledgeably on the *filioque*, affirming its fundamental consonance with the Eastern approach to the Spirit's procession.[27]

Unfortunately, Maximus's irenicism did not catch on. Unsurprisingly then, when in the eleventh century Pope Benedict VIII *did* insert "and the Son" into the Creed, it crowned and confirmed Constantinople's grievances and misgivings about Rome, built up over the centuries. Without denying the import of the theological issue at stake here, the *filioque* controversy always was—and remains still—about much else besides. Contrary to popular belief, the terse phrase "and the Son" did not *itself* cause the "tragic wound"[28] dividing the Catholic and Orthodox Churches. (Much more significant wounding, literally and metaphorically, occurred during the Fourth Crusade of 1202–1204.) Yet the *filioque* clause—and the thicket of historical, political, cultural, canonical, and ecclesiological issues that have grown up around it—illustrates, at least, the centrality of trinitarian teaching within the Christian tradition. Since the Trinity is Christianity's basic summary of *who God is*, and moreover of who God has revealed himself to be, it should not surprise us that Christians have felt the details of it to be something worth fighting over—even sometimes, lamentably, to the point of tearing themselves apart. Though that does not, of course, preclude the possibility that there is—and perhaps even this side of heaven—"a time to sew" (Eccl 3:7) together again.

▲ ▲ ▲

There is one final issue that we must discuss in this chapter: the question of gender. Simply put, the issue is this: The Scriptures appear to present us not just with three divine persons, but with three explicitly *masculine* ones: three "hes." In turn, this gives us an exclusively male-centric set of language and ideas with which to think about, speak of, and above all *pray to* the triune God. True, the second person of the Trinity both became and remains incarnate as a biologically human male. But in what remotely literal sense can the first or third persons—or, for that matter, the second one *prior* to the annunciation—be understood in these terms?

This should, in itself, give us some pause for thought. If God really *is* "above whatsoever we may say or think of him,"[29] then God ought surely to be "above" speaking or thinking of "him" *as* a him. Furthermore, if it is true that all "the big basic concepts in the doctrine of the Trinity...are accepted only inasmuch as they are at the same time branded as unusable and admitted simply as poor stammering utterances—and no more"[30]—and this is a core idea that, even in these brief pages, we have seen expressed by such paradigmatic Christian thinkers as the two Gregories, Hilary, Augustine, Anselm, and Thomas—then it must likewise apply to expressing those concepts in gendered terms. Nor is this a purely abstract point of principle. We need not be naïve about the influences, subtle or not so subtle, that our "interpretation[s] of the things thought about divine nature"[31] can exert on society and culture—especially in those heavily influenced by the ideas, practices, and symbols of the followers of this apparently tri-male God.

Today, it seems an obvious point, even if not to accept wholesale, then at least to consider seriously. The Church fathers' reticence on the topic is conspicuous. Augustine covers a great deal of ground in *On the Trinity*, and here as elsewhere has much to say on matters sexual, and yet God's *own* sex seems not to have piqued his curiosity overly much. Augustine is by no means alone. To modern Western minds, at least, this perhaps appears to be intellectual negligence at best, and like a conspiratorial silence at worst.

▲ ▲ ▲

Looks are not everything, of course. And the early tradition mightn't be as unenlightened as it has, understandably enough, sometimes been considered to be. Certainly, this would be a natural reading of the rare occasions when the question of divine gender *is* directly touched upon. St. Jerome, a contemporary of Augustine's, is a prime example here. In his *Commentary on Isaiah*, he mentions that in the noncanonical Gospel of the Hebrews (a text probably written in the second century, and used by small pockets of Christians in and around Egypt) Jesus refers to "my mother, the Holy Spirit." Now

Jerome could, quite rightly, note here that the text is not Scripture, and has never been accepted as authoritative by the universal Church. Hence even *if* there are things of value in it (and Jerome clearly thinks there are), one must always be alert to the possibility of heretical chaff mixed in with orthodox wheat. However, Jerome says nothing of the sort. Rather, he states simply and anodynely,

> No-one ought to be scandalized in this matter because in Hebrew the Spirit is spoken of in the feminine gender, when in our language [i.e., Latin] the masculine gender is applied, and in Greek the neuter; for in the Godhead, there is no gender [*in divinitate enim nullus est sexus*].[32]

And then, evidently not feeling that he had dropped any great theological bombshell, he moves on.

Still more telling in this regard is a throwaway remark from Gregory of Nazianzus. It comes while he is arguing that "Son" is not a literal biological description, but is used "since we have no other term to express his consubstantial derivation from God."[33] Roundly mocking those who naïvely transpose "human family ties" into the Trinity, he asks, "Do you take it, by the same token, that our God is a male, because of the masculine nouns 'God' and 'Father'? Is the Godhead a female, because in Greek the word is feminine? Is the word 'Spirit' neuter in Greek, because the Spirit is sterile?"[34] It is essential to note here that Gregory feels no need to tackle the idea that either the Godhead in general, or the Father or Spirit specifically (the *incarnate* Son is a special case, of course), can be literally understood in gendered terms. Rather, he is citing the notion here as being so absurd that no right thinking person could possibly believe it, in order to show up the absurdity of a different position entirely. The testimony of Jerome and Gregory, doctors of the Church both, thus strongly suggests something very important indeed. It is not that the Church fathers uncritically accept the idea of a tri-male God. Rather, they consider the idea to be so off the radar that they have a hard time imagining that anyone, even those unorthodox on other key matters, could possibly be troubled by it. Hence, as the *Catechism* puts it, "We ought therefore to recall that God transcends the human distinction between the sexes. He is neither man nor woman; he is God."[35]

▲ ▲ ▲

This does not end the issue, for, in a certain sense, it is just the beginning. If "in the Godhead, there is no gender," then why does the Christian tradition—copying God himself, whose own use of gendered language is amply documented throughout the Scriptures—insist on referring to God in such terms?

Let us consider some alternatives. Avoiding gendered pronouns *he* and *she* leaves us with the neutral *it*. *It*, unfortunately, is known as an *impersonal* pronoun with good reason. It is very hard to love an *it* "with all your heart, and with all your soul, and with all your strength, and with all your mind" (Luke 10:27). Even inanimate objects we feel some kind of connection to tend to get dignified with a personal pronoun. Sailors call their ships *she*, for example; plenty of people refer to their cars, GPS systems, and even iPhones in similarly gendered, personal terms. And though there are ancient precedents for renaming the divine persons in desexed terms,[36] the results are not magnificently satisfactory. Describing them as *Creator*, *Redeemer*, and *Sanctifier* (perhaps the most famous modern example), for instance, arguably depersonalizes the Godhead still further and gestures, albeit unintentionally, toward modalism.

If desexing isn't attractive, then what about resexing? Describing God with feminine language and imagery is on firm ground in terms of both Scripture and Tradition. Both Jerome and Gregory refer above to the fact that the Spirit is, grammatically speaking, transgender: while the Latin *spiritus* is masculine, and the Greek *pneuma* is neuter, the Hebrew noun *ruah* takes a feminine pronoun and article. Also feminine, are the Greek (*sophia*) and Hebrew (*hokmah*) equivalents of Wisdom—a fact particularly relevant in a christological context, as noted in chapter 3 in light of John 1. Obviously, grammar does not make the Spirit or Son literally female, any more than it makes either them or the Father literally male. (Augustine makes one of his very few forays into this field to tell us that "wisdom is not female in sex just because it is called...by a word of the feminine gender."[37]) Nevertheless, it intimates the possibility of envisioning God's nature and activity in feminine metaphors.

This possibility is, furthermore, made an actuality in the sacred page itself. Thus, Isaiah quotes "the LORD, the Redeemer of Israel and his Holy One" (49:7):

> Can a woman forget her nursing child,
>   or show no compassion for the child in her womb?
> Even these may forget,
>   yet I will not forget you.
>
> (49:15)

And slightly earlier,

> For a long time I have held my peace,
>   I have kept still and restrained myself;
> now I will cry out like a woman in labor,
>   I will gasp and pant.
>
> (42:14)

Sirach states simply, "The Most High...will love you more than does your mother" (4:10). In the New Testament, Jesus evokes his desire to "gather [Jerusalem's] children together as a hen gathers her brood under her wings" (Matt 23:37) evincing, as Augustine points out, his "maternal love."[38] These constitute, to be sure, a limited and arguably stereotypical range of exclusively motherhood-related analogies. But the central point remains: the God who "transcends the human distinction between the sexes" may profitably be described in imagery and language drawn from either.

This recognition does not, however, mean that the traditionally masculine-specific language of *Father* and *Son* is somehow arbitrary or replaceable. As detailed in chapters 2 and 3, these, along with the Holy Spirit, are the primary names we have been given for apprehending God by Jesus of Nazareth. Certainly, they are metaphors and thus have their limits; images of paternity and sonship, however rich, by no means plumb the full "depths of God" (1 Cor 2:10). As chapter 1 demonstrates, it is of the utmost importance that we realize and remember this. Yet these are the main metaphors that *God himself*, speaking as "a man among men,"[39] has especially endorsed. They are ones that, whatever their deficiencies when pushed too literally (and Christ himself was even better aware of what those deficiencies are than we are), were surely chosen to be the *least* deficient overall. Putting it bluntly, and adapting one of Gregory's very best put-downs, they were "introduced by a better theologian than you, our Saviour."[40]

All this is most true, of course, in connection with direct commands. Hence, when Jesus states plainly, "Pray then in this way: 'Our Father...'" (Matt 6:9), it is a brave, or reckless, Christian who feels at liberty to start correcting him within the first couple of words. Likewise, while Christ did not give us especially strict rubrics for baptizing, he *did* explicitly tell us to do it "in the name of the Father and of the Son and of the Holy Spirit." That is not an especially demanding script. There is no excuse for not sticking to it.

▲ ▲ ▲

Far more than the other chapters, this one has perhaps felt like heavy going. That in itself is no bad thing. The basic doctrine of the Trinity *itself* is, I will repeat for the final time, simple enough to grasp:

1. There is only one God.
2. The Father, the Son, and the Holy Spirit is each God.
3. The Father, the Son, and the Holy Spirit are not the same.

However, just as maps are not terrains, Christian doctrine is emphatically not the "God of glory" (Acts 7:2). Our faith depends not on words but realities;[41] it is the Word *of* God we follow, and words *about* God only insofar as they help us to meet, know, understand, and love him.

Necessarily therefore, the deeper we explore the Trinity, the darker and harder our way becomes. This is true of the spiritual life in general, of course. Gregory of Nyssa thus imagines Moses's ascent of Mount Sinai to have been a journey into an ever-darkening mystery:

> This is the true knowledge of what is sought; this is the seeing that consists in not seeing, because that which is sought transcends all knowledge, being separated on all

sides by incomprehensibility as by a kind of darkness....When, therefore, Moses grew in knowledge, he
declared that he had seen God in the darkness, that is,
that he had then come to know that what is divine is
beyond all knowledge and comprehension....[42]

As we have had occasion to note many times, the doctrine of the
Trinity is neither more nor less than the Christian understanding of
who God is. Augustine comments, with wry understatement, that
"it is difficult to contemplate and have full knowledge of God's substance."[43] That is precisely why the Trinity is so important.

For nowhere else is a mistake more dangerous, or the
search more laborious, or discovery more advantageous.[44]

Notes

1. Thomas à Kempis, *The Imitation of Christ*, trans. Leo
Sherley-Price (London: Penguin, 1952), 27.
2. Augustine, *On the Trinity*, V, 1. Translation from *The Trinity*,
trans. Edmund Hill (Brooklyn, NY: New City Press, 1991), 189.
3. Ibid., V, 10 (Hill, 196).
4. Ibid., VII, 7 (Hill, 224).
5. Ibid., VII, 9 (Hill, 227).
6. Ibid., VII, 7 (Hill, 224).
7. Gregory of Nazianzus, *Oration* 42, 16. The translation used
here may be found in Philip Schaff and Henry Wace, eds., *Nicene and
Post-Nicene Fathers*, series 2, vol. 7: *Cyril of Jerusalem, Gregory Nazianzen*
(Peabody, MA: Hendrickson, [1890] 1994), 385–95, at 391.
8. Karl Rahner, *The Trinity*, trans. Joseph Donceel (London:
Burns and Oates, [1967] 1970), 57.
9. For example, it hardly seems worlds apart from the sixth-
century philosopher Boethius's definition—"a person is an individual substance of a rational nature"—as quoted by Thomas Aquinas
in the thirteenth century (*Summa Theologiae*, 1a, q. 29, a. 1).
10. Hippolytus, *Against Noetus*, 8. Translation taken from
Hippolytus of Rome, *Contra Noetum*, ed. and trans. Robert Butterworth (London: Heythrop Monographs, 1977), 42–93, at 64.

11. And if so, then the Trinity might arguably offer some
pointed lessons as to how we ought to conduct our own social
arrangements. Most famously, the Brazilian liberation theologian
Leonardo Boff has argued that, properly understood, "the Trinity
can be seen as a model for any just, egalitarian (while respecting differences) social organization" (*Trinity and Society*, trans. Paul Burns
[London: Burns and Oates, 1988], 11).

This kind of "social trinitarian" approach may also be found in
Pope Benedict XVI's 2009 claim that "The theme of development can
be identified with the inclusion-in-relation of all individuals and peoples within the one community of the human family, built in solidar-
ity on the basis of the fundamental values of justice and peace. This
perspective is illuminated in a striking way by the relationship
between the Persons of the Trinity within the one divine Substance."
(*Caritas in Veritate* 54).

12. Tertullian, *Against Praxeas*, 8.

13. E.g., "These three then, memory, understanding, and will,
are not three lives but one life, nor three minds but one mind. So it
follows of course that they are not three substances but one substance." (Augustine, *On the Trinity*, VIII, 18; Hill, 298).

14. Hilary of Poitiers, *On the Trinity*, I, 19. The translation used
here may be found in Philip Schaff and Henry Wace, eds., *Nicene and
Post-Nicene Fathers*, series 2, vol. 9: *Hilary of Poitiers, John of Damascus.*
(Peabody, MA: Hendrickson, [1890] 1994), 31–233, at 45.

15. Gregory of Nyssa, *On Not Three Gods*. Translation from
William G. Rusch, ed. and trans., *The Trinitarian Controversy*
(Philadelphia: Fortress Press, 1980), 155.

16. Augustine, *On the Trinity*, I, 8 (Hill, 70).

17. Gregory of Nazianzus, *Fifth Theological Oration* (or *Oration*
31), 9. Translation from Gregory of Nazianzus, *On God and Christ:
The Five Theological Orations and Two Letters to Cledonius*, trans.
Frederick Williams and Lionel Wickham (New York: St. Vladimir's
Seminary Press, 2002), 123.

18. Ibid.

19. Cf. "But because the Son is 'Son' in a more elevated sense
of the word, and since we have no other term to express his consubstantial derivation from God, it does not follow that we ought to
think it essential to transfer wholesale to the divine sphere the

earthly names of human family ties" (ibid., 7; Williams and Wickham, 121).

20. Augustine, *On the Trinity*, VII, 2 (Hill, 219).

21. Medieval theologians, dissatisfied at not having a technical term to use, suggested *spiration* for the Spirit's own particular way of proceeding (see Thomas Aquinas, *Summa Theologiae*, 1a, q. 27, a. 4).

22. Ibid., 1a, q. 40, a. 2.

23. Tertullian, *Against Praxeas*, 8

24. Augustine, *On the Trinity*, XV, 48 (Hill, 433); cf. Ambrose of Milan, *On the Holy Spirit*, 120.

25. Augustine, *On the Trinity*, IV, 29 (Hill, 174).

26. Augustine, *Enchiridion*, 9. The translation used here may be found in Philip Schaff and Henry Wace, eds., *Nicene and Post-Nicene Fathers*, series 1, vol. 3: *Augustin: On the Holy Trinity, Doctrinal Treatises, Moral Treatises* (Peabody, MA: Hendrickson, [1890] 1994), 229–76, at 240.

27. In detail, see A. Edward Siecienski, *The Filioque: History of a Doctrinal Controversy* (Oxford: Oxford University Press, 2010), 73–86.

28. John Paul II, *Orientale Lumen* 21 (1995).

29. Thomas Aquinas, *Summa Theologiae*, 1a, q. 1, a. 9.

30. Joseph Ratzinger, *Introduction to Christianity*, trans. J. R. Foster (London: Search Press, 1971), 122.

31. Gregory of Nyssa, *On Not Three Gods* (Rusch, 152).

32. Jerome, *Commentary on Isaiah* 40.9; this translation is my own from Jerome's Latin. Origen's mention of the same passage is likewise instructive. His sole focus is on "the difficulty of explaining how the Holy Spirit can be the mother of Christ when it was itself brought into existence through the Word" (*Commentary on John*, II, 6). That is, for Origen the text raises questions concerning the relationships and derivation of the Son and Spirit. Since these would be the same if the text had called the Spirit father or parent, Origen thus betrays no disquiet at the specific "gender angle" here. He promptly solves the issue with reference to Matthew 12:50: 'There is nothing absurd in the Holy Spirit's in the Holy Spirit being his mother, everyone being his Mother who does the will of the Father in heaven' (ibid.).

33. Gregory of Nazianzus, *Fifth Theological Oration* (or *Oration* 31), 7 (Williams and Wickham, 121).

34. Ibid. (Williams and Wickham, 121–22).

35. *Catechism of the Catholic Church* 239.

36. E.g., "Let us speak of the Unbegotten, the Begotten, and the Proceeding, if anyone likes to create names" (Gregory of Nazianzus, *Oration* 42, 17; Schaff and Wace, 391).

37. Augustine, *On the Trinity*, XII, 5 (Hill, 325).

38. Augustine, *Exposition on Psalm 59*, I, 9. The translation used here may be found in Philip Schaff and Henry Wace, eds., *Nicene and Post-Nicene Fathers*, series 1, vol. 8: *Augustin: Expositions on the Book of Psalms* (Peabody, MA: Hendrickson, [1890] 1994), 239.

39. Irenaeus of Lyons, *Against Heresies*, IV, 20, 4. The translation used here is taken from Alexander Roberts and James Donaldson eds., *Ante-Nicene Fathers*, vol. 1: *The Apostolic Fathers, Justin Martyr, Irenaeus* (Peabody, MA: Hendrickson, [1885] 1994), 309–567, at 488.

40. Gregory of Nazianzus, *Fifth Theological Oration* (or *Oration* 31), 8 (Williams and Wickham, 120).

41. Cf. Gregory of Nazianzus, *Oration* 42, 16.

42. Gregory of Nyssa, *Life of Moses*, 163–64. The translation used here may be found in *Gregory of Nyssa: The Life of Moses*, ed. and trans. Abraham Malherbe and Everett Ferguson (Mahwah, NJ: Paulist Press, 1978), 95.

43. Augustine, *On the Trinity*, I, 3 (Hill, 66).

44. Ibid., I, 5 (Hill, 68).

AFTERWORD:
HOW TO BE AN ECUMENIST

Heresy is not, as observed in the introduction, a word too often heard in these ecumenically sensitive times. As also mentioned there, that is undoubtedly for very good reasons. Accordingly, a book that takes heresy and its avoidance as its guiding theme, and even goes so far as to enshrine the "h-word" on its front cover, might be thought not to have been written in an especially ecumenical spirit. This would, however, be a very grave misconception.

Simply put, the doctrine of the Trinity as worked out in these pages is about the most ecumenical piece of Christian belief there is. The very idea of revelation depends upon the conviction that "we cannot speak rightly about God unless God himself tells us who he is."[1] Whatever their other differences, the consensus among the major Christian communities that *Trinity* is an accurate and authoritative shorthand for expressing who "God himself tells us...he is" is impressive. Moreover, the precise way in which the early theologians came to understand and express the idea—three *hypostases* in one *ousia*; three *persons* in one *nature*—is the common and normative heritage for those denominations to which the vast majority of contemporary Christians belong. And along with all this, implicitly or (often enough) explicitly, comes an agreement that the so-called *heresies* of modalism, Arianism, and tritheism really are exactly that: false opinions that deviate from the "correct doctrine," *orthodoxy*, taught and lived by the universal Church. Hence, the patristic rejections of each of these, narrated and explained in chapters 4 to 6, are what today we might call *very ecumenical anathemas*.

The main period we have covered (up until Augustine in the early fifth century), including the landmark Councils of Nicaea in 325 and Constantinople in 381, occurred *before* the main ecclesial splits that persist to this day. It is true that lasting schisms occurred soon after, following the Councils of Ephesus (431) and Chalcedon (451). These were responsible for the independence of the present-day Assyrian Church of the East and the "Oriental Orthodox" family of churches, respectively. In dispute, however, were important points of christological doctrine (a subject for a whole other book); all parties, then as now, affirmed the fundamentals of *trinitarian* orthodoxy.

This is all the more true of the acrimonious divorce between Catholics and Orthodox in the first centuries of the second millennium. The *filioque* issue, important as it was and is, must not obscure the fact that it arose out of—and only really makes sense within—a much broader and deeper agreement on the Trinity. As detailed throughout this book, the defense of the Church's core trinitarian convictions, and the finding of a satisfactory way of "saying all three things at once," was a common cause between Latins and Greeks. Linguistic and cultural differences occasionally obscured matters, but the fundamental harmony between them is, as we have seen, confirmed by no less authorities as Gregory of Nazianzus and Augustine of Hippo, arguably the greatest representatives of "East" and "West."

▲ ▲ ▲

Now, one may perhaps expect claims of a grand ecumenical consensus to break down somewhat in the sixteenth century, with the Reformation. Not so. The Protestants treated many aspects of traditional doctrine and practice with great suspicion, and acted accordingly. But the Trinity was emphatically not among them. Nor, it must be said, was this simply a passive reception of ancient Christian teaching, a purely "formal" acceptance of Nicaea and Chalcedon.

Throughout this book, we, along with the Church fathers that were quoted, have stressed that the Trinity is a thoroughly biblical teaching. To quote again Hippolytus of Rome, "The whole of the Scriptures are a proclamation about this."[2] The key Reformers couldn't agree more. Martin Luther, the champion of *sola Scriptura*, preached powerfully on the subject "of the Holy Trinity, or of the three persons of the Godhead which is the prime, great, incomprehensible and chief article of faith."[3] Naturally, as Luther writes elsewhere, he recognizes that "the name 'Trinity' is nowhere to be found in the Holy Scriptures, but has been conceived and invented by man"[4] (indeed by Tertullian, as we learned in chapter 4). However, he readily admits that "since we have no better term, we must employ [it]."[5] He goes on, with a passage that might just as easily have been written by the Gregories, Hilary, Augustine, or even Thomas:

> This article is so far above the power of the human mind to grasp, or the tongue to express, that God, as the Father of his children, will pardon us when we stammer and lisp as best we can, if only our faith be pure and right. By this term, however, we would say that we believe the divine majesty to be three distinct persons of one true essence.[6]

John Calvin goes even further. He not only agrees wholeheartedly with the doctrine itself, but offers a spirited defense of technical terminology like *persona, hypostasis, consubstantial,* and the rest. Such nonscriptural terms, he argues, "do nothing more than explain what the scriptures declare and sanction"—which is to say, "that three are named, each of whom is perfect God, and yet...there is no plurality of gods."[7] (Note that this is simply a more elegant statement of our trilemma.) Calvin concurs with the fathers that "the unerring standard both of thinking and speaking must be derived from the scriptures."[8] But like them, he recognizes that it is sometimes necessary to coin more exact terminology, albeit "sparingly and modestly"[9] to *protect* the correct meaning of those Scriptures:

> Thus the early Christians, when harried with the disputes which heresies produced, were forced to declare their sentiments in terms most scrupulously exact in order that no indirect subterfuges might remain to ungodly men, to whom ambiguity of expression was a kind of hiding-place.[10]

This, it is worth remarking, is precisely the same argument that Thomas Aquinas makes: "The urgency of confuting heretics made it necessary to find new words to express the ancient faith about God."[11]

Of course, similar examples could be quoted from a great many other leading Protestant writers, from the sixteenth century to the twenty-first. Importantly, such ideas are not simply the personal views of individual theologians, but are enshrined in the binding creeds of a great many of the main denominations. Just two examples will have to suffice here. The Lutheran "Augsburg Confession" of 1530 opens with these words:

> Our churches teach with great unanimity that the decree of the Council of Nicaea concerning the unity of the divine essence and concerning the three persons is true and should be believed without any doubting. That is to say, there is one divine essence, which is called and which is God....Yet there are three Persons, of the same essence and power, who also are coeternal: the Father, the Son, and the Holy Spirit.[12]

Likewise, the first of the Church of England's 1563 "Thirty-Nine Articles"—a central doctrinal statement not just for Anglicans across the world (including Episcopalians in the United States) but historically for Methodists too—states, "There is but one living and true God....And in unity of this Godhead there be three Persons, of one substance, power, and eternity; the Father, the Son, and the Holy Ghost."[13]

▲ ▲ ▲

Naturally, this does not mean that all present-day Christian groups descended from the Reformation are similarly orthodox on matters trinitarian. Nor does it imply that every member of those that *are* subscribes fully, consciously, and comprehendingly to the traditional Christian teaching about who God is. Indeed, this whole book is motivated by the impression that very few committed believers of all denominations—Catholic, Protestant, Orthodox, or whoever—really understand what it is they mean when they, perfectly sincerely, affirm that God is a Trinity. And what is much worse, a very large number of Christians probably do not even think that they either *could* or *should* understand it.

Now this really is, in the words of *Father Ted*, a supremely "ecumenical matter." The Trinity is the preeminent source of doctrinal common ground among the splintered and shattered Christian communities. It is also an urgent topic for catechesis within them all, in order that—to again quote Luther—"this truth of the Godhead may be preserved among Christians, enabling them to know God as he would be known."[14] As I have now stated many times, the word *Trinity* is nothing more or less than the ancient Christian shorthand for expressing the main "bullet points" about who God is, and thus who he has revealed himself to be. As so often, Augustine cuts to the heart of the matter in speaking of "the Trinity, who is God."[15] My primary purpose in writing this book has therefore been, in a very small way, hopefully to help some Christians to "grow in the knowledge of God" (Col 1:10), and to feel confident in helping others to do the same.

By way of a conclusion, permit me—admittedly, a little melodramatically—to make my own Gregory of Nazianzus's words of farewell to the Council of Constantinople:

> Farewell, O Trinity, my meditation, and my glory. May you be preserved by those who are here, and preserve them, my [readers]...and may I learn that you are ever extolled and glorified in word and conduct. My [readers], keep, I pray, that which is committed to your trust....The grace of our Lord Jesus Christ be with you all. Amen.[16]

Notes

1. Joseph Ratzinger, *Gospel, Catechesis, Catechism: Sidelights on the Catechism of the Catholic Church* (San Francisco: Ignatius Press, 1997), 14.

2. Hippolytus of Rome, *Against Noetus*, 14.

3. Martin Luther, *Sermon for Trinity Sunday* (Rom 11:33–36), 1. Translation from *The Sermons of Martin Luther*, ed. John Lenker, vol. 8 (Grand Rapids: Baker Book House, 1983), 7–25, at 7.

4. Martin Luther, *Sermon for Trinity Sunday 1522* (John 3:1–15), I, 1. Translation from *The Sermons of Martin Luther*, ed. John Lenker, vol. 3 (Grand Rapids: Baker Book House, 1983), 406–21, at p. 406.

5. Martin Luther, *Sermon for Trinity Sunday* (Rom 11:33–36), 2.

6. Ibid.

7. John Calvin, *Institutes*, 1, 13, 3. Quoted from *Institutes of the Christian Religion*, trans. Henry Beveridge (Peabody, MA: Hendrickson, 2008), 67.

8. Ibid. (68).

9. Ibid.

10. Ibid., 1, 13, 4 (68).

11. Thomas Aquinas, *Summa Theologiae*, 1a, q. 29, a. 3.

12. Quoted from Theodore Gerhardt Teppert, ed., *The Book of Concord: Confessions of the Evangelical Lutheran Church* (Minneapolis: Fortress Press, 1959), 27–28.

13. Quoted from http://anglicansonline.org/basics/thirty-nine_articles.html.

14. Martin Luther, *Sermon for Trinity Sunday* (Rom 11:33–36), 1.

15. Augustine, *On the Trinity*, I, 7. Note that Hill, our usual translator for this text, gives the more awkward (though also possible) "the Trinity which God is" (*The Trinity*, trans. Edmund Hill [Brooklyn, NY: New City Press, 1991], 69).

16. Gregory of Nazianzus, *Oration* 42, 27. The translation used here may be found in Philip Schaff and Henry Wace, eds., *Nicene and Post-Nicene Fathers*, series 2, vol. 7: *Cyril of Jerusalem, Gregory Nazianzen* (Peabody, MA: Hendrickson, [1890] 1994), 385–95, at 394–95.

FURTHER READING

It is useful to have several books by several authors, even on the same subjects, differing in style though not in faith, so that the matter itself may reach as many as possible, some in this way others in that.

— Augustine, *On the Trinity*, I, 5

Those wishing to read more on the subjects covered, in many cases all too briefly, in these pages are in for a treat. The truly essential texts are, of course, the "primary sources" I have quoted liberally throughout. The Scriptures are, as all my other authors will confirm, the most important of these; I especially advise reading in full the paragraphs, or better the whole books, from which I have only been able to quote short excerpts. Certain passages have, of course, exerted more direct influence than others over the Church's growing understanding of who God is: Genesis 1 and 18; John 1, 14—16, and 20; and Acts 1—2 are the ones to which I especially direct my own students.

Providentially, English translations of almost all of the writings quoted from the Church fathers are freely available online at the *New Advent* website: www.newadvent.org/fathers. These reproduce the *Ante-Nicene Fathers* and *Nicene and Post-Nicene Fathers* editions, first published in the late nineteenth century, pleasingly well-thumbed copies of which can often be found on theological library bookshelves. I have made much use of these translations myself; they are often the only English ones (cheaply) available. There are, however, a few newer and zippier versions of some key texts that are worth seeking out. The main ones I have used, and I fully recommend reading in full, are listed below:

William G. Rusch, ed. and trans. *The Trinitarian Controversy.* Philadelphia: Fortress Press, 1980, including, among much else, letters by Arius, Alexander, and Eusebius of Caesarea; significant chunks from key writings by Athanasius and Gregory of Nazianzus; and Gregory of Nyssa's *On Not Three Gods.*
Hippolytus of Rome. *Contra Noetum.* Edited and translated by Robert Butterworth. London: Heythrop Monographs, 1977.
Gregory of Nazianzus. *On God and Christ: The Five Theological Orations and Two Letters to Cledonius.* Translated by Frederick Williams and Lionel Wickham. New York: St Vladimir's Seminary Press, 2002.
Augustine of Hippo. *The Trinity.* Translated by Edmund Hill. Brooklyn, NY: New City Press, 1991.

Thomas Aquinas has also been a frequent and welcome guest on these pages. His *Summa Theologiae*, in the 1920 translation published by the English Dominicans, is also available online at *New Advent* (they *really* do do good work): www.newadvent.org/summa/.

In addition to deeper engagement with the original sources, readers will surely profit from a firmer grounding concerning the historical contexts out of which those texts and their authors emerged—topics, fascinating in their own right, but necessarily skated over in a work such as this. There are many interesting, reliable, and intensely readable accounts of early Church history. Of these, I highlight just a couple of treasures, old and new (cf. Matt 13:52):

Henry Chadwick. *The Early Church.* Harmondsworth: Penguin, 1967.
Morwenna Ludlow. *The Early Church.* London: I. B. Tauris, 2008.

Finally, my own learning, thinking, praying, teaching, and writing concerning "the Trinity, who is God" (Augustine, *On the Trinity*, I, 5) has been guided and enriched by a great number of modern writers. I am most conscious, however, of owing a debt to the following authors and books:

Edmund Hill. *The Mystery of the Trinity.* London: Geoffrey Chapman, 1985.

Gerald O'Collins. *The Tripersonal God: Understanding and Interpreting the Trinity.* Mahwah, NJ: Paulist Press, 1999.

Karl Rahner. *The Trinity.* Translated by Joseph Donceel. London: Burns and Oates, 1970.

Joseph Ratzinger. *Introduction to Christianity.* London: Search Press, 1971.